Aid Matters

A Book of Cries, Questions and Prayers

'Charity corrupts giver and taker alike; and, what is more, (charity) does not attain its objects as it only increases poverty' (Dostoevsky).

AID MATTERS

A Book of Cries, Questions and Prayers

Alec Gilmore

Dear Myra

This book goes as a token
of our sincere appreciation
for all you did for Eclof

in friendship

Cees Oshm

SCM PRESS LTD

Copyright © Alec Gilmore 1998

0 334 02717 9

First published 1998 by
SCM Press Ltd
9-17 St Albans Place London N1 0NX

Printed in Great Britain by
Redwood Books
Trowbridge, Wilts

CONTENTS

LENT

HOLY WEEK

EASTER

EASTER TO PENTECOST

PENTECOST

POST-PENTECOST

Excellence Unnoticed — Questions Unasked

This book is primarily about aid and secondarily about literature and communication. It springs from a desire to demonstrate different ways in which literature affects the lives of people in the developing world, the wide spectrum of problems and opportunities it brings to light, and the variety of gifts which are therefore needed to respond to it.

It is an attempt to portray some of the excellence in the developing world which too often goes unnoticed and to raise some important questions facing the West which too often go unasked.

It has been compiled because there is a constant demand for resource material for those who preach, teach and lead worship, because aid and the issues associated with it are an important and regular part of that diet, and because stories and information relating to literature and communication, though crucial, are often hard to come by.

What we understand by aid

For many people, aid is fundamentally a mixture of poverty, starvation, refugees, wars and natural disasters.

At its most popular level, and among people who have neither time nor inclination to stop and think about what is happening, interest in aid is fed by television pictures, mainly in news bulletins, by 'cheap' radio adverts inviting you (cajoling you?) to 'send a fiver to granny' or 'buy a school book for a child', or by the worst expressions of the big aid agencies simply begging for money.

Among the more thoughtful and educated, thanks in part to the 'weightier' press but much more to the regular campaigns which have been going on in the churches for the past 20-30 years, and to a few academic strongholds, like the Institute of Development Studies in Sussex, the problems are increasingly recognized as global rather than individual, development rather than charity, and debt rather than aid.

The cry for literature

With all these problems, many of them literally matters of life and death, it is hardly surprising that the cry for literature (let alone *Christian* literature) is scarcely heard. The squeak of a mouse amid a herd of stampeding elephants!

To many (to *too* many!) it means sending Bibles and possibly hymn books — and even then, usually old ones which nobody here could use any more. Next, it means tracts and evangelism — many have still not come far from 'converting the heathen' though they would no longer put it in those words. Next may come the tools of Christian education (if we are in the churches) and more general books for schools (if we are not). Only for a few is the cry for literature for the developing world a serious recognition that participation in an increasingly literary global environment requires not only the basic capacity to read but also access to the world's literary treasures, new and old, and at all levels.

An organization committed to addressing these issues in the developing world shares all the problems of the aid world in general, and often, because it is smaller, less pressurized and more focused, is in a better position to see them and appreciate both their urgency and their complexity. Agencies which concentrate on literature and communication are also aware how often literature is the 'search engine' or the driving force without which nothing moves for long, if at all. The 'search engine' may be a small part of the WWW and the 'literature search engine' may occupy only a small space on the aid lorry, but its significance is out of proportion to its size, and long-term success depends on giving every attention to its maintenance, research and development — though that is not necessarily what it gets!

Perhaps the literature agencies themselves are in part responsible. Some have been too content to concentrate on immediate relief rather than long-term issues, and even those who don't have not always been clear how literature and communication needs fit into the overall aid programmes. The connections are not always immediately obvious. Sometimes we have spelt them out, but not always, and indeed part of the exercise is encouraging others to make the connection. Nevertheless a few remarks may help.

Take for example one agency which developed a project for latrines in one of the poorer countries of Africa. To every Western eye there was no doubt about the need and to most agencies no reason to question the wisdom. The money was forthcoming without any difficulty. The problems only came to light twelve months later when an aid worker went back to see how things were going. The latrines were still there, almost in pristine condition. Fine. The only problem was that nobody was using them. People found it easy to disappear into the woods. They might be going there for all sorts of reasons. But no self-respecting man would run the risk of his mother-in-law seeing him go into the latrines. So what looked to a Westerner like a simple problem of hygiene turned out in fact to be a matter of communication — or the lack of it!

Or take the remarks of Dr Alan Kirton, General Secretary of the Conference of Caribbean Churches, addressing nearly 200 representatives in London from Catholic and Protestant missionary societies who were looking for ways in which British churches could 'think global' and 'act local'. (The remarks were made in 1986 but the underlying issues have not changed in the meantime.) He said,

'There are three things in Britain which have angered West Indian Christians.

One, your government's failure to respond positively to sanctions over South Africa.

Two, the sacking of cricketers Viv Richards and Joel Garner.

Three, the failure of one senior British government official to remember every speaker's golden rule. *Think before speaking.* As a result he succeeded in giving the impression that all West Indians were idle lay-about good-for-nothings.'

On the surface, hardly aid and development issues, yet the failure to see the connection is itself part of the problem. Our failure to communicate speaks volumes about how we feel and proclaims from the housetops our lack of perception. On the surface, hardly a literature issue either, until you pause to appreciate the gap between what was said (or done), what was *reported* in the Caribbean, and how what was reported was *received.*

Literature (and other forms of electronic communication) so often represents the ways and means by which needs are first made known, assessed, felt, and responses made. Witness, for example, the use of everything, from photocopied news sheets and street drama through to the press and full-blown theatre. Perhaps it is only when we appreciate the part literature plays in our own life, including our history, society and culture, that we become more acutely aware of its importance for others, which means that unless we do something similar for the Third World in addition to their basic bread and butter, food and clothing, they will be deprived of making the same discoveries and responding to them for themselves. Hence the need in a book like this to address such broader issues as human rights, torture, theatre and so on.

Finally, literature which is a true reflection of life enables us to see ourselves and to make more informed choices and more meaningful responses. Some societies will always need help in creating that literature just as others need grants for arts and the theatre.

PLAN AND CONTENT

The contents are of several kinds.

1 *Biblical base.* A starter or theme for each section, followed by a reflection to avoid going to the same passages for aid issues and to encourage the discovery of basic aid issues in other places.

2 *An essay.* An attempt to highlight a common error, misunderstanding or misuse of aid, to provide resources for further study, factual information, suggest a new line or stimulate thought. A useful starter for a study group or issues to raise in preaching.

3 *Stories.* A variety of anecdotal material from 'the literature front' in the form of human stories, incidents, quotes, new pieces of work, problems being faced, people involved, etc, to highlight issues, humanize and personalize what is going on, provide a corrective for much we take for granted, and arouse feelings which may lead to confession, thanksgiving and intercession.

Though most of these stories relate to particular individuals or groups, they are not isolated incidents or people. They are typical. They are not intended to be used just as they are, but rather to create interest, stimulate thought and prayer, and lead readers to make discoveries for themselves. Similarly, the sketches under 'The Cutting Edge' and 'The Changing Face' are included to increase awareness of the issues and stimulate readers to explore similar territory.

4 *Worship.* Bible readings and reflections, prayers, suggestions for further reading, and pointers to comparable secular material as a further aid to devotion and meditation, and things to do.

The book is planned on the basis of the Christian Year and the content selected largely with that in mind. At the same time most of the material is very flexible and, with minor changes, could be used on almost any occasion.

I have tried to steer a middle way between a collection of material with no obvious connections and a minimum of direction and a tightly structured book which may well have deprived readers of seeing and discovering connections for themselves. I hope I have got it about right, and that people who need the links I have provided will find them helpful, whilst those who do not will enjoy taking off '*my* labels' and allowing the various pieces of text to respond to the varying contexts and speak for themselves.

Two further difficulties were how to be specific, personal and authentic without breaching confidence, and how to avoid dating.

I have handled the breach of confidence by changing names or inconsequential details, by not being too specific about location, or (where necessary) by getting permission.

'Dated material' was a bigger problem. The situation in a developing country changes more rapidly that in a more stable society and organizations can be there today, doing splendid work, and gone tomorrow. For this reason a book cannot supplant a leaflet put out by aid agencies for a particular Sunday and is not meant to. I have tried to overcome this in two ways:

1 Where the details mattered less than the ongoing issues I have tended to generalize, whilst at the time making clear that the specific did exist and probably still does, though perhaps in a different place and with different people.

2 Where material is clearly dated (eg Chile or Eastern Europe in the late 1980s) I urge users to appreciate and concentrate on the nature of the problem rather than the details, but to use the detail to enter imaginatively into the needs of the people then and now, and then to find something similar in today's world.

ADVENT
A Time to Stop and Start Again

Theme

. . . it stands written:
I am sending my herald ahead of you;
he will prepare your way.
A voice cries in the wilderness,
Prepare the way for the Lord;
clear a straight path for him.'
John the Baptist appeared in the wilderness proclaiming a
baptism in token of repentance, for the forgiveness of sins.

Mark 1: 2-3 (REB)

John the Baptist's cry is an invitation to people who have never thought they were perfect but who have always had a deep sense of privilege and a basic feeling that in general they were on the right lines.

If you were going to issue a cry for repentance (or change of heart and mind) there were surely many people to whom it ought to be addressed before the Jews. They were certainly doing more of the right things than some other nations they could mention.

But John the Baptist had a different sense of awareness. It was those who were most sure of themselves, or who took their position for granted, who most of all needed to stop and think again.

Those who have led the world in colonialism for close on 500 years, who take a pride in parliamentary democracy or promote their country as the bastion of the free world, and who go further than most to fulfil their responsibilities to the Third World, are the very ones who need again to hear this call.

key word	*metanoia* is (literally) 'a change of mind'. Repentance is not simply recollecting what we have done wrong and being sorry, though that is part of it. It is also

μετανοια

Repentance

a change of mind	seeing things differently
a change of heart	cultivating different feelings
a change of direction	actually doing things differently

And one way of hearing this call is to observe others who have heard it, see what it meant for them and how they responded.

The Third World — Who Needs Whom?

Next time anyone calls to collect your Christian Aid envelope try asking them whether the Third World really exists, whether (if it does) it really needs our money or whether in fact it might all be a mistake because the Third World is nothing more than the creation of Western governments as a means of giving foreign aid. It might be like challenging the set speeches and programmed responses of Jehovah's Witnesses, but these are real questions not to be dismissed.

First, the name (Third World). Nobody really knows where it came from and nobody finds it satisfactory. One person traces it back to the 1920s when there was talk of finding 'a third way' between capitalism (First World) and socialism (Second World) but few people over sixty have any recollection of hearing it in their youth. Another view traces it to the 1940s, when Asia, Africa and Latin America were lumped together as the under-developed world, and a third states categorically that it was a post-war creation of the West, a necessary part of the West's economic structure and entirely the result of the West's need to transfer funds overseas.

During that time it has served its purpose in more ways than one.

Sometimes it has proved a convenient way of dividing the world into two, keeping oneself on the side of the angels and clearly identifying the enemy — a collectivity confronting the West and (as a collectivity) hostile to it. Sometimes, it is a shorthand way of distinguishing between rich and poor, white and coloured, north and south, donors and receivers, stagnant economies and buoyant economies, developed and developing.

And though there has been widespread dissatisfaction with 'the Third World' as an omnibus description of what we are talking about and many alternatives have been put foward, such as the undeveloped world, the less-developed world, the developing world, the non-aligned world, the South, and the Two-Thirds World, none has ever found universal acceptance and none has succeeded in removing the stigma that gave rise to the change. A rose by any other name still looks like a rose, smells like a rose and pricks like a rose!

So how did it come about? In popular estimation, the Third World is a mixture of poverty, colour, race, exploitation, under-development and disasters, but the facts hardly support the presentation.

The divide is not one of rich versus poor. It is just not true that the First World is rich and the Third World poor. Very large parts of the West are manifestly not rich and it is possible to find some rich countries such as the Middle East, South East Asia and Latin America in the Third World category. Not all individuals even in the rich countries are rich, and there are some excessively rich individuals in some of the poorest countries.

Nor is it a matter of stagnant economies versus buoyant economies. The West is not universally buoyant nor the Third World universally stagnant. Indeed, some Third World economies, such as Taiwan, Singapore and Brazil, are far from stagnant and one economist (Meier) claims that since 1950 even *per capita* incomes in the Third World have on the whole grown no less fast than in the West, and probably even faster.

Nor has it much to do with exploitation or skin colour. The only thing all the countries lumped together as 'the Third World' have in common, it is argued, is that they are all recipients of foreign aid. 'The concept of the Third World and the policy of official aid are inseparable,' says Meier. 'Without foreign aid there is no Third World.'

If that view is right (and not all economists would agree with it) then it moves aid from the realms of charity or development into the realm of politics. In fact (so the argument goes), it suits Western governments to have it that way. To call the transfer of billions of dollars of Western tax payers' money 'foreign aid' or 'overseas aid' or indeed 'aid' at all disarms criticism. It is a convenient way of handling both aid and trade, and if not intentionally a way of blurring the lines it is at least at times a way of not striving officiously to keep them apart. At the same time it controlled some fears and anxieties by creating a strong group of neutrals during the Cold War. In the eyes of others, particularly in the Third World, it has been seen as a political way of assuaging Western guilt for colonialism.

Unfortunately, one effect of turning charity into politics has been to prejudice the effects of the policy, to obscure its realities and results and to contribute to the politicization of life in the Third World. At the same time it has given strength to the churches, who saw their limited attempts at charitable relief being given credibility by the backing of government aid. At the same time they could argue that the real issues were political and therefore it was necessary for them to get involved in the political struggle by becoming part of the development lobby.

Neither churches nor politicians were particularly good at assessing or evaluating the effect of their policies overseas, whilst their Third World partners, who find it difficult enough to be involved in what is happening to their projects even when they are developing them and seeking funding for them, found that at this level of policy they had no share at all. Truly, the creation of the West.

And why do we do it? Is it only because we find it convenient to lump two-thirds of the world together and treat it as one? Or is it because we can then treat 'the Third World' as 'them', which is better? And how long will it take us in the West to get used to living without the Eastern block countries in Europe or apartheid in South Africa? Must we have either an enemy or a dependent? [1.1]

The West has tried to apply its own conceptions of 'development' to the Third World, working through local élites and pretending that the benefits showered on these élites would trickle down to the less fortunate, especially through the wholesale application of Western-inspired and Western-supplied technology. These methods have not produced a single independent and viable economy in the entire Third World — and in fact were not meant to. 'Development' has been the password for imposing a new kind of dependency, for enriching the already rich world and for shaping other societies to meet its commercial and political needs. [1.2]

'Imperialism' out! 'Globalization' In!

The word 'imperialism' no longer exists. It has been banished from the dictionary and replaced by 'globalization', which 'suggests a world community of interest and means the opposite'. It is administered primarily by the great banks with their 'structuralist adjustment' programmes, one consequence of which is that the poor countries have 'loans for projects they don't need and debt that kills them.'

'Each year half a million children die as a result of the attempts by poor governments to pay the interest on loans', according to the UN Children's Fund. [1.3]

REPENTANCE IN RUSSIA

In the late 1980s *perestroika* and *glasnost* were on everybody's lips. Two other Russian words which came very much to the fore *there* but never quite made the same impact *here* are *miloserdiye* and *dukhovnost*. Both have to do with a change of heart and mind

MILOSERDIYE

For seventy years *Miloserdiye* was almost banned in Soviet society, excised from the dictionary with the word 'obsolete' beside it. Then, around 1990, it bespattered the pages of the press. What does it mean?

In Hebrew it is *hesed*. In Greek it is *charis*. In Latin *caritas*. In the revived churches of the Soviet Union it meant the revival of a caring society, springing from the church with the blessing of the state. But it was more than a revival. It was a change of heart and mind.

Michael Bourdeaux traces the change to 1986 with the explosion at the power station in Chernobyl. It was far too big a disaster for the Soviet authorities to conceal and yet the state had nothing like the resources to match the scale of the disaster. So for the first time in seventy years the churches found themselves engaging in a direct caring ministry with the state behind them. Together they raised three million roubles for the victims, and the Baptist churches in Kiev opened their doors to provide temporary accommodation.

Floods in Georgia and an earthquake in Armenia served only to intensify the campaign, and despite some opposition the churches found themselves setting up schools, hospitals, children's and old people's homes. Miloserdiye Societies appeared in twenty major cities. In Rostov they started a Miloserdiye Week.

It was a change of heart and mind for the state. It was a change of heart and mind for the churches. It is not clear who repented first, but it is clear that in both cases it opened the door to a new future.

DUKHOVNOST

The fruit of that repentance is *Dukhovnost*. It has been translated 'quality of spirit', but it is much more than the West understands by 'spirituality'.

Dukhovnost is 'all that happens in your life when God is the central point of reference' and is perhaps best understood in terms of what it achieved.

Dukhovnost made prison visits a regular part of the churches' programme. One Christian said it was the first time in seventy years that a priest had visited a labour camp except as an inmate.

Dukhovnost made visits to hospitals, psychiatric clinics and old people's homes an everyday activity, often to help out in times of staff shortage. The director of one hospital said patients needed the support of faith and love, the sort of compassion you get from believers. In another, patients were even asking to be assigned to those wards where they would be cared for by Baptists.

Yet most of these Christians had grown up in a world where they had never known what it was to be able to apply their faith outside the narrow confines of the church structure, and even that only with restraint.

But if change of heart and mind did that for the believers it also did something for the state. In a world where hundreds had been imprisoned for teaching basic Christian standards to children and where conditions in children's homes and boarding schools were appalling in the extreme, the state was now actively looking for Christian homes to which deprived children could go. [1.4]

AFTER REPENTANCE — WHAT?

If we were able to change our way of life what might it look like?
One possibility can be found in the Maya of Guatemala

The Maya are a different people with a different set of basic values, where ecology was 'in' before it was in fashion.

The Maya are one of the great culture-nations of Central America who occupy what is now the Republic of Guatemala and surrounding areas. Second only to the Mexicans, they can claim to be equal to them in material and intellectual civilization and in other ways even surpass them, though they are much less well known when it comes to their history, civilization and daily life. They were the great astronomers and mathematicians of their day with an elaborate system of hieroglyphic writing, not yet fully deciphered, though their main method of communication was oral and pictorial rather than literary.

Today the Maya are anxious to convey to their children the values of natural life and respect for humanity because they believe that in creation we are at the very heart of heaven and earth. It is here, in trees and flowers, birds and wild life, that we meet God. But we meet him too in storm and tempest, fire and flood, sun, moon and stars, and indeed apart from all these things we are unable to touch him.

Yet, believing this, they are aware that many in the West call them idolaters. They say it is because in the West we have no understanding of Maya philosophy, no relation with the natural, nor with the personal, much less with the heart of heaven and earth, because our god is a commercial god, a god of power and money — and that for them really *is* idolatry.

In Maya thinking woman and man are a reflection of the living God: a God of life, full of love. That is where they find a concern to give, to care, to protect and to defend life.

For the Maya, ecology has always been important, long before it became fashionable in the West and not only because of conservation. For the Maya, a tree is a personal life. Cut it down and you strike not only at the heart of heaven but also at Mother Earth. When it comes to water, the tree has a lesson to teach us: it uses every drop and does not waste any. In both trees and water God gives life and comes to us in concrete form, whilst animal and bird life also communicate to us in other ways what it is to be human. Not by the usual patterns of aid and development. That is to become part of the problem or at least to connive at it.

Life in Guatemala today is particularly tough and makes most Western efforts at conservation look like a cake walk!

Government oppression can be very heavy-handed and this adds insult to injury with an already overwhelmed suffering Indian population. On the occasion of a recent international conference, the Secretary of the Council of Churches and his family had to flee the country within twenty four hours in order to survive, and even then representatives from the international conference had to go to the scene in order to safeguard his life and that of his family.

In Guatemala suffering is a daily experience for everyone. For the Christian church the work is always painful and the reality of the cross ever present.

PIGS OF CLASS

In the West we live in tension between the world as we enjoy it and the world as we would like it to be. Repentance may mean doing something more than 'feeding the ducks from the river bank'

Around Easter 1996 George Monbiot reported on an outbreak of African swine fever which started in Dominica and spread to Haiti. It killed about one-third of the pigs, but the American authorities could take no chances so they slaughtered them all to be on the safe side.

For the peasants it was catastrophic. Their small, black pigs were their main source of income. The word for 'pig' was the same as the word for 'bank'. Not to worry, said the US. They could now replace the little black pigs with big white pigs and become a major exporter. What they did not say was that the new variety needed a lot more attention than the old, and before long the pigs were enjoying better accommodation and more showers per head than the peasants.

Gradually, the black ones 're-appeared', but were frowned on by the Americans, and by 1994 they had succeeded in just about destroying the Haitian peasant economy by buying up their lands to grow coffee and flowers to export to America.

> 'If we do not . . . discourage these developing countries from aiming at self-reliance now, our world-wide competitive position will continue to slide.' (US Senator) [1.5]

Such developments were but one stage in the Green Revolution, a policy of introducing new crops to Third World countries in order to avert the famines which had been threatened in the 1960s, engineered, funded and promoted largely by the USA, which just happens to be the world's most aggressive food exporter. But a report from the International Food Policy Research Institute revealed that though more calories were being consumed, nutrition-related diseases (such as iron, zinc and vitamin A deficiency) had either remained unchanged or increased. New varieties lacked some of the critical nutrients present in the crops they replaced. Farmers, the report suggested, should go back to the varieties they were growing before, though possibly with increased yields.

Other 'victims of the Green Revolution' suffer from soil erosion, pesticides, water shortage, indebtedness, declining incomes and an unhealthy dependence on expensive farm imports. [1.6]

'As peasant producers are knocked out by bankruptcy and ecological collapse, farming all over the world is concentrating in the hands of those who can afford to invest in the most lucrative crops — luxuries for the First World rather than necessities for the Third. This trend could scarcely suit the First World better. We get cheaper fruit, flowers, coffee and sugar as well as new markets for our surplus grain.' (Monbiot).

Aid workers are warning of a major famine in NW Haiti because of drought. Children are already dying of hunger and 350,000 people could be at risk if there is no substantial rainfall in the next two weeks. The US is ready to send in more food aid, but a US charity has warned that American aid is undermining efforts to increase local food production. [1.7]

A BIBLICAL PERSPECTIVE

Micah saw similar changes taking place in land ownership in the eighth century BC. An agricultural community from its earliest times, land had always been important to Israel. In the early days of the settlement they had to take what they could and naturally some did better than others, but for the most part they fought it out 'on a level playing field'. Come the monarchy, however, and the growth of a rich élite that went with it, and land in the fertile valleys became more desirable than land on the hillside. Powerful people had the opportunity to take it, and they did. The weak began to go to the wall.

Better land then meant better living. The discovery of iron meant better tools for those who could afford them. Better tools meant better results. Better results meant more money. More money saw the beginnings of a market in luxury goods. All of which could have been so wonderful because everybody could have benefited from the prosperity. Instead, those who had it kept it for themselves and then to their selfishness added corruption. Increasingly, the powerful took the fields, then the homes, then the women and the children for slaves.

The powers-that-be could, of course, have done something about it. They could have regulated it even if they couldn't have stopped it altogether. They did neither. Instead, they joined in. Micah says they treated people as if they were sheep for slaughter (3: 1). What inflamed him most of all was that it was not just the king and the rulers but also the judiciary and many of the prophets who were parties to the injustice and gave no sign whatsoever of 'biting the hand that fed them'. Yet the change was so gradual and so subtle, that the only people who seemed to notice were the victims and they were the last group who could do anything about it. What he saw made him a Liberation Theologian.

CAN WE BEAR THE PAIN?

Thanks to the air traffic which required the destruction of the market gardens on which Heathrow was built, we can now enjoy apples, potatoes and coffee from places as far apart as France, South Africa and New Zealand, all the year round and at a price we can afford.

Or would it be more correct to say 'at prices we can pay'? George Monbiot questions whether we can afford them. We only think we can because we never 'cost' them.

What price the 'command economy' of the superstores? Quite apart from annexing the food market and fixing standards, prices, conditions and wages overseas, they move into other spheres like banking and enjoy privileges when it comes to buying land and securing developments, often backed up by alleged 'benefits to the community'.

But what price local produce, local shops, local diversity? Jobs, houses, transport and pollution? Is it a price we can afford? Or would we rather not ask the question? [1.8]

HITTING BACK?

Attached to the theological college at Tobelo, Halmaheera, in Indonesia, there is a training centre where students can learn such practical matters as carpentry and animal care — all very important for ministers working in a rural environment.

I enjoyed looking at the rabbits and the chickens but never bargained for the comment I got when we came to the pigs. Most of them were black. Suddenly my guide's eyes lit up and he said with considerable enthusiasm, 'We've got some more pigs over here — a gift from Germany. Come and see. They look just like you!'

I hope all he meant was that they were white!

WATER IN INDIA

A Doctor has a Change of Mind — and then a Change of Direction

In 1960 an Indian in Maharashtra, Dr Gujur, was one of four medical doctors with a concern for rural medicine and no funds. Their first plan was to start a hospital, but they had all manner of setbacks and three of them gave up. Dr Gujur alone remained. Within seven years he had established a different institution.

His first change of mind came in 1970 when he started looking outside the hospital. If he were really to heal these people he needed to know a lot more about the causes of their complaints. He knew so little of their social environments. What were they eating and drinking? What sort of houses were they living in? What were the local conditions like and what were their problems other than health? And so on. So he turned the whole hospital into a health centre, and his change of mind became a change of heart.

He developed a new concern and a new commitment to the people. He observed that as long as you related to planners, development workers and aid experts they talked of roads, most likely because they wanted to get to the village. And when the first farmer said that what he wanted was not roads but water everybody thought he was crazy. But the people who actually live in the villages have a more basic understanding of what the real need is.

It was then that he decided to change direction. He moved from hospitals to wells. He set about helping farmers in one valley with irrigation problems, as a result of which malnutrition was considerably reduced, living conditions were changed, and by moving on to the wider needs of agriculture and food supply they were able to bring new life and a new level of self-sufficiency to many people.

This is now the kind of resource Dr Gujur is trying to give to others. His aim is to improve people's basic economic life-style by providing the resources they need rather than the resources aid officials think they ought to have. It isn't always wells. In another project, working among tribal people, it was bee-keeping and harvesting medicinal plants.

'It's something to do with priority,' says the doctor. 'If you have only £10, what can you do to help and make sure that you still have £10 at the end of it?'

Of course such projects still require aid and cannot of themselves be self-sufficient, but once they are developed and the health of the people improves, the whole community achieves a new measure of independence.

More important than whether a project is self-sufficient is whether it helps the people to self-sufficiency.

'When I feed the poor, they call me a saint; when I ask why the poor have no food, they call me a communist' (Helder Camara)

DIRT IN INDIA

A Civil Servant has a Change of Direction — and transforms Life for Thousands

In 1996 an Indian civil servant, S. R. Rao, cleaned up the slums of Surat and set in motion similar forces as far away as Delhi, Bombay, Calcutta, Madras and Bangalore. It was the plague that did it.

Less than five years ago unattended animal carcasses, rotting in the streets after a flood, accounted for the deaths of 58 people and though medical treatment saved the rest the lesson was learned.

It wasn't only the flood. Surat is a city of 2.2 million people and growing at an annual rate of 6.6%. Less than a third had drains. More than half had no access to tap water or toilets. Rubbish rotted where it fell.

Today, access roads and drains have been installed in the slums and 95% of the rubbish is collected daily. Surat is one of the cleanest cities of India and is being copied by others.

Rao denies he is a social reformer. 'I am not', he says; 'I am a paid civil servant.' But he has brought about a transformation of life for thousands.

First, he simply enforced existing regulations and applied them scrupulously to rich and poor alike. On-the-spot fines, drains, pay toilets, street lighting and rubbish bins.

He then made city sanitation employees spend half their working day in the fields — a voyage of self-discovery as they rubbed shoulders with people whom normally they would never meet.

He took on manufacturers who flouted sanitation regulations and built illegally on government land. They rebelled at first, but either by reason or a few strong-arm tactics he won them round.

Now people are proud of their city and deaths from communicable diseases in the poor areas are down by 50%. [1.9]

LIBERATION THEOLOGY — a Practice long before it became a Philosophy

For centuries the church in Latin America was incapable of distinguishing between evangelization and enslavement. There were honourable exceptions — priests who spoke out against atrocities committed in the name of God — but they were seldom heard. Today, while many senior churchmen continue to absolve repression, bishops and priests throughout the continent have sided with the poor.

Seeing that there was little virtue in trying to help the poor without confronting the exclusion and exploitation making them poor, the pastors began to use the Bible to show people why they were oppressed. Citing Luke 4:18, they helped to establish some of the most robust labour, land and housing movements in the world. Millions, who would have lost their livelihoods, owe their survival to the new theology. [1.10]

GUATEMALA TODAY . . .

Guatemala has more Protestants than any other Latin American country. Most are fundamentalists, but there is a Conference of Evangelical Churches with a programme of theological education which aims to promote a genuinely Guatemalan theology by reflecting on the meaning of Christianity and the purpose of life in their situation.

For the first time ever it has brought together Mennonites, Presbyterians and Methodists, as well as some other smaller communities. The members are mostly genuinely Indian churches, many of which have actually broken away from the white-dominated churches because of the discrimination they have encountered.

ALFALIT, a Latin American literacy organization, has worked hard among the Maya on literacy and literature programmes of a different kind over many years. Their main concern has been with the needs of new readers, particularly women.

But in Guatemala (and indeed in many other parts of Central America) you cannot be interested only in the art of reading. If you are hungry and you have no work and no hope of getting work, what are you learning to read for? And what are the texts which help you to read?

Over the last fifty years there has been both criticism and anxiety among Christians about Communists providing literature for people in poor countries. Less has been said about the same rôle when performed by oppressive capitalist landlords and employers so as to keep their tenants and workforce in slavery.

So it is not surprising that ALFALIT, which is committed most to those in most need, weighs in with the Maya on the side of Justice, Peace and the Wholeness of Creation, which in turn means an emphasis on learning to respect the world and nature, and working together for the good of all creation.

. . . and ISRAEL IN THE TIME OF MOSES

Just over sixty years ago an Arab, ploughing his bit of land in the far north west of Israel, struck something hard. It was a box containing some clay tablets and the archaeologists were called in. As it happened there was nothing of note there but then the archaeologists noticed a nearby hill which looked as if it might be interesting. It was. It was the ancient city of Ugarit, destroyed about 1200 BC, with a temple, a palace, and thousands of manuscripts all written during the previous 300 years.

This was about the time that Moses and the Children of Israel were entering Canaan. These tablets tell us about the religion they found there.

The 'king of the castle' was called El, the Creator. More important was the second in command, Baal, the God of wind, and rain and climate. That was

what mattered to these ancients. Half of them were agriculturalists: it mattered that the rains came at the right time and they had a good harvest. Their livelihood depended on it. The other half were fisherfolk: it mattered to them that the seas were held in control for the safety of their ships as well as for finding their food. Baal was important, not only for religion, but for survival.

Was this perhaps one of the ways in which first the Jews and then the Christians came to believe in a God who was concerned with the whole of life?

It doesn't necessarily mean he always controls everything for *us*. He has to care about other people's needs as well as ours! And perhaps what matters is not what happens to us — to any of us — but how we respond.

POVERTY AND THIRD WORLD DEBT

In many countries poverty cannot be tackled until the burden of debt is lifted

If you think loans to poor countries are acts of generous kindness by rich countries

    remember it suited the West
to make the loans in the 1970s
to earn interest for itself
on otherwise idle capital.

If you think debtors should repay their debts

    remember that many countries
have long since repaid the money
they originally borrowed
but interest rates have shot up.

If you think government aid goes to help the poorest in Africa

    remember that over half of it is used
to repay rich creditors like ourselves
in a crazy money-go-round.

If you think poor countries should get on their bikes and earn their keep

    remember that African countries have
increased their exports by fifty per cent
and could have paid their way
if prices on the world market had not fallen.

If you think this is all economics and has nothing to do with our faith

    read what the Bible says about
selling the needy for a pair of shoes
and putting the last first
and debt forgiveness and justice
and good news for the poor
in the year of God's Jubilee. [1.11]

In 1993

sub-Saharan African governments

paid £169 million more

to the IMF than they received

THE CUTTING EDGE

Certeza Argentina, a Buenos Aires-based, non-profit-making organization, which publishes and distributes Christian literature for Argentina, started, like SCM and IVP, with a mission to provide informative books on Christianity for students.

While making available translations of classic contemporary Christian titles, Certeza Argentina considers the development of Latin American authors its chief task and of the 80 titles published since 1984 half were written in Latin America.

On a continent dominated by the didactic and rote-learning techniques of both the Roman Catholic Church and North American fundamentalism, Certeza Argentina committed itself in the early 1980s to 'the inductive method of Bible teaching', encouraging people to ask questions and to apply the Bible to daily living.

The first Certeza bookshop opened in 1980 in Buenos Aires and continues to be a strategic distribution centre with other Certeza bookshops in two of the suburbs. While bookselling is fully self-financing and publishing pays its own running costs and overheads, some external funding is still needed for capital, training, special projects and new technology.

Certeza Argentina has a director, editor, marketing manager and designer (all part-time), supported by a board and editorial committee made up of volunteers from different professional and church backgrounds with a common commitment to Christian literature.

As Argentina's only ecumenical book publisher, Certeza is in a unique position to support the church and society by promoting deeper dialogue among Christians and a biblical analysis of the political, social and spiritual reality.

THE CHANGING FACE

St Andrews Biblical Theological College, Moscow, is an independent teaching institute which capitalized on the increased liberty offered in the late 1980s and started its own publishing house.

Like many similar institutions in Eastern Europe, the College had to publish its own resources because of the shortage of biblical and theological material in Russian, because publishers are few and far between and often unwilling to handle Christian literature, and because printers can make more money publishing other things.

They now have two magazines, *The World of the Bible*, the first illustrated magazine on biblical theology and hermeneutics to be published in Russia, and *Stranitsy*, meaning 'The Pages', a journal which documents the college's weekly seminars on Theology, The Church and Culture, and The Church and Education. It will also be used in the college's correspondence courses.

The college has two full time and twelve part time staff whose sole task is to publish new theological texts for students and to promote the distribution of Christian literature.

Sadly not all the hopes for religious freedom have been fulfilled. Some former KGB officials who worked on the abolished Council for Religious Affairs are now 'advisers on church-state relations' in the provinces and some provincial governments have passed laws against religious freedom and human rights.

A Light for the Gentiles

Alongside John the Baptist's call to repentance (addressed, remember, to God's 'chosen people') reflect on Simeon's judgment that Jesus is to be 'a light to lighten the Gentiles' (Luke 2: 32). Advent is a preparation for Incarnation. Incarnation has to be about humanity and not about one particular race or group. So consider how a chosen people feel, think and react when they realize that their 'chosenness' is not necessarily for them alone.

1 Trace Simeon's words back to their origin in Isaiah (42: 6; 49: 6), where Isaiah's understanding of Yahweh as the God of more than Israel, and Israel as a nation with a mission, is being worked out, and how it is placed in a context where the suffering of the Servant (whether it be an individual or the nation) is never far away (Isaiah 42: 1-4; 49: 1-6; 50: 4-9; 52: 13-53: 12).

2 In Jewish thinking the Gentiles denoted everybody who was 'not one of us'. So who are 'the Gentiles' for us?

3 Ponder the different ways in which the English versions put a gloss on Simeon's words, so reflecting different attitudes to 'other people' and the way we feel about God's dealings with them.

Are they 'pagans' or 'heathens' to be enlightened by truth which has already been vouchsafed to us (JB, NEB)? 'Outsiders' who still lack the knowledge of God's will which we have been privileged to receive (GNB)? And are they 'others' to whom something has to be brought (REB) or is the light something they may well discover and appreciate for themselves and in their own way (RSV, NRSV, NIV)?

Try to evaluate on a scale of 10 how much the attitude of 'the faithful' to 'the others' has changed in 2,000 years and then sort out in what ways. Simeon's words have much to say to us about how we in the West see the developing nations and respond to them, and also how we respond to many 'others' in our own society.

Understanding this during Advent, hearing John's call to repentance and responding to it could make all the difference to our appreciation of Christmas.

Silver and Gold

Advent is also a time for the preparation of gifts. Gifts may be of two kinds: those we give because we love (John 3: 16) and those we give because people need (Exodus 16).

Reflect on the differences between the two alongside Peter and John, accosted by a beggar, on their way into the temple (Acts 3: 1-10).

1 Think of this beggar not necessarily as someone who needs money but as someone who begs for money. We don't know whether he needs it. We do know he needs health. But he begs.

Identify people like him in today's world. They may sleep on the streets. They may cry to us from Ethiopia. They may be on a trade mission from Zambia or trying to negotiate some overseas aid with the Foreign Office. What they all have in common is that they are asking for money.

Poor people, whether sleeping in Trafalgar Square, struggling in the shanty towns of Brazil, or trying to raise the resources for an operation because the waiting list is so long, either assume that money is the solution to their problem or have come to the inevitable conclusion that the cry for money is the only cry likely to be heard by those who have made it their god. They never ask for anything else because they have given up believing that anything else might be forthcoming.

2 Identify the Peters and Johns — the people with resources to whom the cry is addressed. Giving money is often the easiest and simplest thing to do. Easier to throw a coin as we walk along the street than to take time off to work out what

politically needs to be done to remove the problem. Easier to donate a million than to change your trading policy if you are a giant supermarket.

3 Penetrate the mind and heart of Peter and John to work out why their response was different. Accept the fact that it had to be, because they had no money. But would they have given money if they had? And would they have been right to do so? Or does their negative response invite us to consider whether the way we use Christmas as a focal point for generosity to the poor and needy may be blinding us to something more important that the festive season is trying to say to us?

Jeremiah's Field

Midway between Moses and John the Baptist came Jeremiah. Jeremiah grew up under the shadow of the fall of the northern kingdom, and though there had always been talk of its revival it had never happened. Now Judah faces something similar. Overrun by the Babylonians and with the cream of the land carried into exile, life is at its lowest. What 'the others' had always known the chosen people are beginning to experience. The promised land is disintegrating even before their eyes.

Read and reflect how in that crisis Jeremiah went out and bought a plot of land (Jer 32: 1-15). Ponder the details carefully and see how much you *feel* belongs to today.

In a day of total darkness he thought he saw a glimmer. Not because he thought everything was going to be all right. He knew disaster was coming. Nor because he had faith in his country's leaders. He had no time whatsoever for the alliances which they were trying to build up with Babylon. Nor because he felt there was going to be a revival of old-time religion. He knew the old religion had not worked and was indeed partly responsible for their present plight.

Ask a few questions to clarify the basis of his hope and see if you can identify similar signs today.

Was the source of his hope that he had faith in people — their ability to stop and start again? Could he perhaps see that when the political leaders had done their worst and moved on to other things, and when everything around him that he valued had been destroyed, the heart of the common people would revive? Did he feel that, however long it took, once they began to ask the fundamental questions they would come up with some totally different answers?

This would then be something written on their heart, an expression of their personal integrity. They would establish a new covenant and something new and better would emerge (Jer 31: 31-4). That is his message of hope. Advent is about hope.

Things to Do

SEVEN STEPS TO CHRISTMAS

The run-up to Christmas is ridden with conflicting emotions:

— a desire to do the best we can for those we love

— a thrill from the lights and the shops and what they offer

— a sense of guilt that we have so much and waste so much

— a feeling we ought to do something about the poor of the world.

But what about the poor at home?

1 Look closely at 'Poor Statistics', visit the library and bring them up-to-date.

2 Comb the press, radio and TV. Keep your eyes open as you drive the car, sit in the train or on the bus, cross the street or go shopping. Put human faces to faceless figures.

3 Organize a few friends to do the same exercise and meet shortly before Christmas to share your experiences.

4 Try to feed some of the your thoughts and feelings into services of worship leading up to Christmas.

5 Keep them at the front of you mind when you sing the hymns and hear the familiar stories.

6 Make sure that the human faces behind the figures appear regularly in the churches' prayers.

7 After Christmas meet with your friends again to talk about the difference it made to you as persons and to your feelings about Christmas.

If you wish to do something positive for the poor around you as a result, fine. But don't feel you have to or the guilt will come on again. There is some value in simple perception. Time will do the rest.

POOR STATISTICS

In Britain and the US the rich are getting richer and the poor poorer. The same is true all over the world and the gap is getting wider. It doubled between 1960 and 1980.

In 1980, the richest 20% received 82.7% of the world's total income. The poorest 20% received 1.4%. Ratio: sixty to one!

After 1980 it got worse. The real wages of the poorest fell and their services deteriorated..

From 1981-87 the lowest non-agricultural wages in Latin America fell 41% and indicators of social welfare in Africa — such as nutrition and access to doctors — sank below their levels in colonial times.

By 1990, more than 1.3 billion people lacked access to safe drinking water, 880 million adults could not read or write, 770 million had insufficient food for an active working life and more then a billion lacked even the most rudimentary necessities.

Meanwhile, the North (25% of the world's people) steams ahead to consume 70% of the world's energy, 75% of its metals, 85% of its wood and 60% of its food.

It used not to be like this. In the 1750s living standards in the North were not notably higher than in the South, which means that in just over 200 years the average citizen of the capitalist world has become eight times richer than one in the non-capitalist world.

Nor is it all thanks to our skill, technology and know-how. A lot of it is due to draining wealth from the under-developed periphery to the developed centre.

Not very different from the old imperialist exploitation of the weak by the strong!

Food for Thought — Food for Prayer

OUR LITERARY WEALTH

Imagine lying in bed on a Saturday morning. You don't have to get up. How many books can you see in your bedroom, and how many different kinds of newsprint, cassettes, etc?

Leave your bedroom and go downstairs. Have you passed any books on the way? Go into your living room. Any books there? Daily paper? Go into the kitchen? Books? And not only cookery books? Go to church. How many books and pieces of paper are stuck in your hand?

How often in the course of a day do you pass a book shop or a newsagents, a music shop or a library? How many other shops have leaflets, literature, etc. to offer you? And so on . . . and so on. We live in a wealth of print and music, books, magazines, etc.

Classify them as in a library. Extend the list to include categories you haven't got. Visit the library to extend the list further.

Give thanks for the wealth, and remember those who have none, and those for whom even a piece of paper is at a premium.

In each prayer section we will focus on one category but always be prepared to add your own.

Category

Bibles, Prayer Books, Daily Readings and Devotional Writings

Remember

Bible translators, preachers, scholars and all teachers of religious education

Focus On

your favourite writer, text or Bible passage and give thanks for the written word

---

LATVIAN BAPTISTS

Give thanks for a small community of Latvian Baptists — about 5000 members, 50 churches and as many ministers — struggling to re-build their Church (and churches) since independence.

— for a large 4-storey building, confiscated in 1945 and returned in 1990 to form the basis of a Seminary — a handful of students and a few thousand books, some new and some old but hardly a comprehensive library.

— for some good Macintosh computers for desk-top publishing (a gift from Southern Baptists), the skills to use them, a few books already published and a magazine which any church in the West might be proud of.

Pray for their encouragement and for professional training for their staff, especially in the English language, the second language of Latvia and the first language for theological study.

Pray for Writers and Composers

who use their skill and experience

to enable us to see what we might otherwise miss

to hear what we might otherwise fail to notice

to understand what otherwise we may find incomprehensible

and to feel what otherwise may pass us by

CHRISTMAS AND THE NEW YEAR
A Time to Travel

Theme

In those days a decree was issued by the Emperor Augustus for a census to be taken throughout the Roman world . . . . Everyone made his way to his own town . . .

Luke 2: 1, 3 (REB)

In some respects Christmas is the last time to travel, especially in the northern hemisphere. It's cold. It's dark. The days are short and the nights are long. Over any journey there is an air of uncertainty. And so it was in the beginning. There could be no joy in the journey for Joseph and Mary, yet law (if not custom) required them to travel and to be with their own kith and kin.

The question they had not yet begun to address was who were their kith and kin, and when it arose it did so in painful circumstances (Matt 12: 46-50), no doubt poignantly reminding Mary at least of Simeon's words thirty years earlier (Luke 2: 35).

Today, in some respects, of all the Christian festivals Christmas is the one when we find it easiest to identify our kith and kin — the poor and the powerless. No room at the inn — homelessness.

The baby — weakness. Mary — the single parent. Herod — the tyrant. The Shepherds — the workers. The Wise Men — gifts from those with something to give. And so on.

Never mind that intellectuals have questioned just about every detail of the narrative. It persists. It lives in popular estimation. It sets the scene for the Man for Others, as well as for much of today's theology, missiology and charity.

But the gospel is not an invitation to summon up pity. It is an invitation to identify with him as he has identified with us. One way of doing that is to travel into the hearts and minds of the poor, not to see if we can change them (i.e. bring them to repentance) but more to see if their struggle can change us. Then *we* can repent.

key word	*eskenosen* comes from *skene*, meaning 'tent'. It is a temporary dwelling, sometimes used metaphorically of the 'body' providing a temporary dwelling for the soul.
ΕΣΚΗΝΩΣΕΝ Tenting	And just as Jesus's 'tenting' was temporary so ours will be also. We cannot live other people's lives. We cannot even identify with them every minute of our existence. The spirit of Christmas cannot last for ever. But in that moment of identification change can take place which can affect everything else. We can then return to our country by another way.

The Travel Fallacy

Aid Agency representatives and tourists all travel. But is there any difference? And how much do they see, hear or understand?

There is a popular fallacy that First World tourism is a good thing for the Third World. Instead of indulging oneself on the sun-tanned beaches or sailing single-handed across the ocean, why not make a sacrifice and go and see how the other half lives? It appeals to some for their honeymoon as being 'something different'. And we like to think that when we get back it will be easier to enter into *their* situation and understand *their* problems.

There are also economic considerations. It's cheap! But then travellers spend money so it must be good for Third World economies. Tourists buy gifts so it must be good for cottage industries busily producing them. Conferences, often held in Third World countries to keep down costs, can be justified on the grounds that it helps the country and gives people 'a chance to see what it is like', especially if they can arrange a one-day trip to 'see the sights'. Churchgoers justify their trips on the grounds that they make partnerships of lasting value, and church leaders and aid agency operators on the grounds that they are offering support.

But when all is said and done, does foreign travel really help Third World countries?

Some of the severest strictures come from within the professional world of aid and development and are directed at rural development tourism, especially by foreigners and journalists. To begin with, rural development itself is something of a Cinderella. It is so much easier for aid workers, not to mention aid agency representatives, to operate in the urban environment. It is safer, cheaper, more accessible — and there is more to do in the evenings! Cut your teeth in the rural areas if you must, but

once qualified there are plenty of other places needing your attention.

But then one day, for a variety of reasons, the call comes and a rural project needs investigation. The journey will be undertaken but everything will conspire against it. It probably has to be in the dry season, so that limits what you see for start. It may have to be organized in a party. That limits it more. Participants probably have little knowledge of rural life even at home; that limits not only what they actually see but also how they perceive it. Difficulty of access may limit who can actually go, and it is likely to be short because not too many visitors want to hang about there. Finally they probably know from the start what they are looking for and therefore will want to find it as quickly as possible and get back to 'the real world'.

Yet in spite of all that, of which the rural people are well aware even before the delegation arrives, the locals will put on the best show of hospitality they can and so ensure that the picture is distorted further.

Gone are the days when Christian missionaries almost buried themselves for life in such situations and so earned the right afterwards to talk about it, and failing that everything else should be taken with caution.

So do Third World people fare any better from straightforward tourism to more popular areas? Not much, if at all. In many cases the resources 'enjoyed' by the tourists will belong to a foreign owner, the major costs will be paid in their own currency before they leave home and any financial benefit to the Third World will be slight. And if the aid agency representatives are encapsulated when they visit the rural area there is no word to describe the limitations which will be placed upon the tourists' perceptions as a result of their travels. One writer has called it 'a mobile ghetto' (Ron O'Grady). Of real life in the Third World they may see little or nothing at all except insofar as it penetrates the walls of the hotel to provide service or as they gaze out through the coach window.

If they are sensitive to the Third World (allegedly the reason for undertaking the trip in the first place) they will be acutely embarrassed when the coach stops to allow them to take pictures. If they buy a few baubles or examples of local produce when the coach stops at the gift shop on the way home they will wonder how much of what they spend actually gets into the hands of the people who have produced it. If they are well informed, they will want to ask how much the local crafts and skills have actually been destroyed in an attempt to create only the things which the tourists are known to favour, and in a colour and in a style that tourists will buy.

Not only have we changed their products. We have also changed their life-style, culture, dances, music, jobs and relationships as they have come to see that to please is to pay, and they need what little money they can get, even if the rewards of tourism for them are pitiable. Small wonder they are not enamoured of the tourist who comes in a package.

Of course, there are a few sensitive tourists, at all levels, but they are a tiny minority and any good they do is more than countered by the damage done by the rest. Nevertheless, tourism has come to stay. Its effects on the Third World will continue. But is that a reason for making it respectable? There must be 'a better way of travelling'. [2.1]

No man should travel until he has learned the language of the country he visits (Emerson)

EXTRACT

A sketch to illustrate the problems of a visit by an aid agency representative

The visitor sets out late, delayed by last minute business, by colleagues, by subordinates or superiors anxious for decisions or actions before his departure, by a family crisis, by a cable or telephone call, by others taking part in the same visit, by mechanical or administrative problems with vehicles, by urban traffic jams, or by any one of a hundred forms of human error. Even if the way is not lost, if there is enough fuel and no breakdowns, the programme runs behind schedule. The visitor is encapsulated, first in a limousine, Landrover, jeep or car, and later in a moving entourage of officials and local notables — headmen, chairmen of village committees, village accountants, progressive farmers, traders, and the like.

Whatever their private feelings . . . the rural people put on their best face . . . Speeches are made. Schoolchildren sing or clap. Photographs are taken. Buildings, machines, construction works, new crops, exotic animals, the clinic, the school, the new road, are all inspected . . . There are tensions between the visitors' questions and curiosity . . . Time and an overloaded programme are nevertheless on the officials' side. As the day wears on and heats up, the visitor becomes less inquisitive, askes fewer questions, and is finally glad to retire, exhausted and bemused, to the circuit bungalow, the rest house, the guest house, the host's official residence, or back to an urban home or hotel. The village returns to normal . . . When darkness falls . . . the visitor is not there. [2.2]

A BETTER WAY OF TRAVELLING

It is not practical for everyone to travel to be with the poor at Christmas.
But we can all use the festival as an occasion to travel 'in head and heart'.
This is the time when Jesus became 'one with us' —
it is the time for us to become 'one with others', if only for a season

When Joyce Grenfell was in South Africa she found herself being chauffeured by a young black African of twenty-five called Nicodemus.

She asked him where they were and he said it was the University. Then he added, 'Education is a wonderful thing'. He had not been able to finish his because the family's money ran out but he said he had read many books.

'What kind of books?' she asked him. Somerset Maugham, Stefan Zweig, Chekhov, Guy de Maupassant, and others. He belonged to a Methodist Reading Club. They all read the same books and then went to discuss them with a wonderful teacher.

Together they chatted of the possibility of understanding through reading. Then he said, 'I am going to many places in books. All the time I am travelling in my head.' The phrase stuck.

Back in London Joyce Grenfell made a song out of it using drum beats as an accompaniment, two in the left hand against three in the right, with the middle verse as a chorus.

She performed it first in the Yvonne Arnaud Theatre in Guildford and assigned the copyright to Feed The Minds because of their interest in Third World books. [2.3]

TRAVELLING IN MY HEAD

I cannot leave my country,
I cannot get a pass to go away.
Money is something you must have also
And money is something I do not have today.
But I am making a discovery:
Right where I am are books and books,
And books are full of people and places
And wide new ideas and poems
On love, and other subjects,
And I am going away, away,
I am going away — in books.

All the time I am travelling in my head,
All over the world I am going,
I am travelling in my head
And I am knowing different people,
Different history,
Different thinking — different mystery,
And people, people talking —
All the time I am travelling in my head
Making discovery.

Johannesburg is my city,
I drive a big car for a business man.
Waiting is something I must do often
And when I am waiting I am reading what I
        can.
Since I am making my discovery
More I am reading books and books,
And books are full of terrible stories
And wonderful visions growing
Of man and what he can be,
And I am going away, away,
I am going away — in books.

When the Tourists Flew In

When the tourists flew in
our island people
metamorphosed into
a grotesque carnival
— a two-week sideshow.

When the tourists flew in
our men put aside
their fishing nets
to become waiters
our women became whores.

When the tourists flew in
what culture we had
flew out of the window
we traded our customs
for sunglasses and pop
we turned sacred ceremonies
into ten-cent peep shows.

When the tourists flew in
local food became scarce

prices went up
but our wages stayed low.

When the tourists flew in
we could no longer
go down to our beaches
the hotel manager said
'Natives defile the sea-shore'.

When the tourists flew in
the hunger and the sqalour
were preserved
as a passing pageant
for clicking cameras
— a chic eye-sore!

When the tourists flew in
we were asked
to be 'side-walk ambassadors'
to stay smiling and polite
always to guide
the 'lost' visitor . . .

Hell, if we could only tell them where we really want them to go! [2.4]

Ten Commandments for Tourists

1 Travel in a spirit of humility and with a genuine desire to learn more about the people of your host country.

2 Let your sensitivity to the feelings of others prevent you from taking their photographs without permission.

3 Do not expect special privileges.

4 Take care that what enriches you neither robs nor violates others.

5 Acquaint yourself with local customs and discover the enrichment of seeing a different way of life through other eyes.

6 Do not make promises unless you are certain you can keep them.

7 When you bargain remember that the poorest merchant would sooner give up his profit than his dignity.

8 Remember that time concepts and thought patterns different from your own do not make your hosts inferior, only different.

9 Cultivate the habit of listening and observing, rather than merely hearing and seeing.

10 Do not waste money travelling if all you want is 'a home from home'. [2.5]

BALI AND BUSES

'The flow of tourist buses through local villages and peasant areas often becomes an unpardonable invasion of privacy. Traditional societies are resentful when someone takes photos of them without permission. In Asian places it is seen as stealing a part of their psyche.

Call to mind the familiar picture of the tourists leaning out of the windows of the bus to take photos with a tele-lens of women bathing in a river or villagers cooking their meal on a fire.

Then picture for ourselves the reversal of this process. Imagine a group of foreign people, wearing strange clothes, speaking none of the local languages, trespassing into the gardens of a house in London, New York, Sydney or Stuttgart, peering through the windows, and taking photos with tele-lens of the husband washing the dishes or the wife in the bath.

In Western society people would be shocked and scandalized and would call the police. Yet this is precisely what tourists in the Third World are doing day after day.' [2.6]

'A curious little picture can be drawn around the custom of dress. In traditional Balinese society, women were always naked from the waist upward but the whole of the lower half of their body was covered by a full-length sarong. When the Europeans began to arrive, a combination of Puritanism and uncertainty resulted in social pressures which led the women of the island to cover their breasts with a blouse. One of the cultural niceties which was completely unknown to visiting foreigners was that Balinese men had rarely seen a woman's ankle or the lower part of the leg, because of the long sarong. The short dress of the visitors was offensive to the Balinese women and stimulating to the local men. Just as Western young men find bare breasts titillating, so the Balinese young men find excitement in the forbidden sight of women's ankles. On the Balinese roads you see Western young men on motor-bikes travelling to the remote villages to watch the beautiful Balinese women's upper torso and passing Balinese young men driving their down from the hills to sit at the beach and watch the young Western women's lower torso.' [2.7]

FOOD FOR THOUGHT

'A bastard is a child born of an illicit relationship. The bastard does not belong fully to either parent.

Out of tourism is born a bastard culture, and one parent leaves without accepting any responsibility for the child left behind.' [2.8]

Tourism injects the behaviour of a wasteful society in the midst of a society of want. [2.9]

If you really want to travel, stay at home. [2.10]

BEACHES, CULTURE AND ENVIRONMENTAL DAMAGE

There are three things the tour operators and travel films never tell you. One, the smells. Two, the bugs. Three, the damage you may be doing to the local people and their environment

Samuel Johnson said, 'To travel is to regulate imagination with reality'. Jean Keefe says, 'Tour operators profit from selling dreams and try to ensure that reality never encroaches on fantasy'.

Beaches

You may dream of tropical climates with sandy, palm fringed beaches, beautiful scenery and exotic life. Luxury hotels may create an illusion of paradise. But it is all very far removed from the reality of local people.

In many cases, in the Caribbean, it was the building of these hotels which pushed up the price of land, dispossessed the peasant farmers and contributed to the mass migration movements of the 1960s. Once there the best beaches belonged to them. Local people could no longer enjoy them. And because tourists were overwhelmingly white, negative racial attitudes were reinforced and Caribbeans made to feel like second-class citizens. Yet Caribbean governments encouraged local people to keep the tourists happy.

Much the same story in Tunisia. Luxury hotels and holiday villages are virtually self-sufficient. They provide little benefit for local residents because the tourists rarely leave the complexes to spend money in the local community.

Nude sunbathing tourists offend local people in Sri Lanka, and as prostitution increases Sri Lankans fear the sort of sex tourism they see in Thailand.

Local Culture

Tour operators have a virtual monopoly of information. Few promote local culture, art, food and history. When they do it is often in a negative and insensitive way. Tourists, as a result, show little respect for local customs and traditions.

Those Tunisians whose natural life is in caves in the hillside find their homes invaded by coachloads of tourists and some have even felt obliged to surround their caves with barbed wire to protect their privacy.

Environmental Damage

Rapid growth of tourism can lead to environmental damage, pollution and a shortage of fresh water. Travellers in Tunisia have swimming pools, superb cuisine and hot and cold showers in every room. Many local people travel miles to collect water from wells. Very few have access to running water or electricity. Meat is scarce and expensive. Few Tunisians can afford it. Yet the average tourist in Tunisia eats more meat in two weeks than the average Tunisian eats in a year.

When destinations fail to live up to their reputation and decline in popularity tour operators take their business elsewhere and leave the locals who have invested scarce resources in attracting tourists even more impoverished.

Far from reducing the gap between rich and poor tourism more effectively highlights the contrast between the tourists and the local people. [2.11]

JOURNEY OF A CHILD

From Islam to Christianity — and a literature ministry

My story begins with the Christ-child (or was he just a child of God?) setting out with his father one dark night on a donkey, escaping from one world which he knew full well to another world which he scarcely knew at all. Like Jesus going down into Egypt he was unable to understand all that was happening and the clear vocation which lay before him.

A BOOK OR A BOOK TOKEN ?

Readers still struggling to find something for Uncle George for Christmas are quite likely in the end to settle for a book or a Book Token. In either case there will be plenty of choice. It will probably be in English (what else, silly?) and produced by an English publisher.

But if Christmas is to be a time of entering into other people's experiences, it may be appropriate to remember those parts of the world where every book is at a premium and often non-existent. Nor is it only a question of poverty.

What Bishop Hassan did in Iran has been attempted in many other countries, with similar successes and failures.

Like the Wise Men, also travelling from the East in search of the Christ, he remembers gazing up at the night sky, so beautiful in that part of the world, with the early morning light on the gorgeous mountains, and reciting to himself the opening verses of Psalm 8: O Lord . . . how majestic is thy name in all the earth. . . when I look at the heavens . . . what is man . . . ? And so on.

The time was the early 1930's. The country was Persia (now Iran). The boy's name was Hassan, and he later became Bishop Hassan Dehqani-Tafti.

Hassan came to Christianity through his mother and his grandmother. Before 1914 his grandmother had eyesight problems and there was a Christian hospital at the nearby town of Yezd. His mother took her for treatment. Grandma became a patient and mother became a nurse. So the gospel was preached in Hassan's home before he was one year old, and at the age of four he can remember crowds of people coming to his mother's dispensary. She was the one person to whom everybody brought their problems. Before he was five she had died of TB, pleading with the Christian missionaries to see to it that the children were brought up Christian. Their father was a Muslim.

So began a constant friendly battle between Hassan's father and the Christian friends of his mother. So too began a conflict within Hassan between the rival claims of the two faiths. And on the night he left on that donkey he was escaping from the world of Islam to embrace the world of

Christianity, in a new school 200 miles away in Isfahan. The conflict continued until eventually at eighteen he was baptized into the Christian faith and never looked back.

On two crucial occasions in those years Hassan's father had consulted the Qur'an and both times he had received the answer Hassan wanted, though the boy knew that had his father opened the book a page or two this way or that the result might have been very different. In all this Hassan saw the hand of God using the Qur'an just as 2,500 years before Isaiah saw the hand of God in the activities of Cyrus the Persian emperor.

By the early 1940s, when he was ordained, he had acquired a taste for literature. He took that quotation from George VI's Christmas broadcast ('I said to the man who stood at the gate of the year . . .') and translated it into Persian, which subsequently found its way into the Persian hymnbook. Twenty years later, having by then become the first Persian bishop, he decided to do something to give his people Persian books by Persian writers.

Once or twice during the 1960s, attempts to create an Iran Literature Association had failed, but in the early 1970s Bishop Hassan made a direct appeal to the West for funds and laid the foundations for the Iran Literature Association. Seven churches were involved, a feat of co-operation in itself. There was also co-operation in Europe. The CMS offered a couple of missionaries and the Danish Missionary Society a third. Some of the cash came from Feed the Minds.

The result was two thriving bookshops in Tehran, a third, even more successful, in Isfahan and at one stage plans for a fourth of Ahwaz.

To develop publishing took longer, but by the late 1970s children in Iran had the religious Ladybird titles and other Bible story books in their own language, church members had their daily Bible reading notes, and expatriates could buy a copy of *Teach Yourself Persian*.

Changes in Iran in the early 1980s put a stop to most of the good work, many expatriates who had been working on these programmes had to leave the country and the Bishop himself went into exile. In this case the Wise Men were not able to return by another route and Herod had his way with the young child. But it is still only one chapter in the saga, and the end of that story which started under the stars of a dark Persian sky has yet to be told. [2.12]

Journeys in My Mind

When Terry Waite was asked how he managed to survive being held hostage for four years in intolerable conditions, he replied, 'I used to make journeys in my mind'.

Being a good Anglican, he could remember many of the services in the Book of Common Prayer. So he used to imagine himself in a church he had visited — a tiny village hall, a cathedral, at home, in Africa or wherever — and he would say, 'I am joining you today', and then he would recite the service.

Meditation

Direct your sight inward and you'll find
A thousand regions in your mind
Yet undiscovered. Travel them, and be
Expert in home-cosmography.

William Habington (seventeenthth century)

12,000 BIBLES . . .

'Today being Sunday I'm sorry we are not able to give you a Bible. Since this campaign started we have given out 12,000 Bibles, and we still have some in the warehouse but we have none here. And we can't get in the warehouse on Sunday.'

An American preacher, addressing thousands of Russians in one of the largest assembly halls in Moscow, right in the heart of the Kremlin, within a few months of the downfall of Gorbachov. His organization had booked the hall for a couple of weeks. Then, having made their impact, they were to continue somewhere smaller and less expensive.

First the choir — to set the mood. Then the Bible — ten to fifteen minutes of the most basic Bible introduction. ('On your lesson paper you will see a reference to the Old Testament and a page number. You find that at the beginning of your Bible.')

Slowly he took us through three passages and then introduced us to the greatest text of all — John 3:16!

Next came the doctor. 'Time to give thought to our anxieties and tensions.' The brain. The slides were incomprehensible, the overhead projector inadequate for an audience of that size, and the teaching method unsatisfactory, but we had to learn about the pituitary gland, and how important it is to our emotions and lifestyle, etc.

Whatever made Russians go to this every night? 'They're going for the Bibles', my Russian friend said. 'Every time they go they get their card punched. So many punches equals one Bible.'

But were Bibles in such short supply? Not really. There were plenty in the shops. But they did cost about 60 roubles and Russians had other things to spend their 60 roubles on.

. . . and 2,000 HYMNBOOKS

'We are a group of young people just back from the West Indies. When we went to church we were horrified to find such a hymnbook shortage — six people sharing one book! So, since they use our old book and we are spending money on new ones, why not send us your old books and we will get them where they are so badly needed.'

The letter in a Christian newspaper bears all the marks of youthful enthusiasm. What the writers did not know, and those who did were reluctant to tell them, was that those same churches had a plan to produce new books. They were just about to purchase printed sheets, bind them, sell them at a price people could afford, boost their income and maintain their dignity all at the same time.

Instead, old books poured in, many totally unfit to send anywhere, until the figure topped 5,000, by which time somebody cried 'enough is enough',

donors were asked to stop sending and the Caribbeans intimated that 2,000 was the most they could handle, mainly because they wanted to sell their own edition compiled from those unbound sheets they had agreed to purchase but which now, with a market flooded by old books, they could no longer make profitable.

So some donors who had been led to feel they were doing something useful had wasted money getting them to the collecting point, and that, plus all the other costs of the operation, would have gone a long way to enable the West Indies to buy what they wanted for their own production.

At the same time, by depriving the church of the chance to produce new books and sell them, it will be even more difficult for the church through its publishing to produce more books once they are needed in the future.

HAPPY ENDING

'Somebody else has got there, or that's what it looks like.'

The speaker was a busy church executive who had pulled out all the stops to supply some books to a church they were twinned with in Eastern Europe. The bill was well over £2,000 and just when he was about to settle the bill he discovered that some other organization seemed to have paid the same amount for the same job. Not surprisingly, he didn't like it.

That was in the early 1990s when things were opening up in Eastern Europe. Western Europe was falling over itself to help and the poor Easterners were so overwhelmed they didn't quite know what had hit them. Everybody wanted to give them something so they simply asked everybody who came along for what they wanted.

His mistake was that he had failed do his homework. Had he been a bit more alert or experienced he would have looked more carefully at what he was being asked to do. He might have checked to see whether anybody else had been asked to do the same. He might have taken advice from a few agencies who specialized in that field. It wouldn't have been easy, but with only a moment's thought he might have realized what he was walking into.

He was fortunate. At this point he told a specialist in the field and a few discreet enquiries soon revealed that they had indeed had a large assignment of the same books paid for by another agency but had sold them and were now were seeking another edition. Clearly a cause worth helping. A chance to build on something which had already proved itself.

So a very much relieved executive was glad to know that he had an answer if anybody started asking questions. But he could have saved himself so much trouble and embarrassment if only he had thought in the first place. Perhaps next time he will.

RUSSIAN BAPTIST EDITOR SPEAKS OUT

'Too many Western businessmen, including publishers', he says, 'come rushing in. They are all interested in doing their own thing and when they realize they can't, most of them rush out just as quickly.

Even Western churches are not beyond criticism. Again and again, I come here and sit round the table with someone from the West. There is lots of sympathy and not a few ideas. The right things are said — and then they go away and we never hear any more about it!'

✳ ✳ ✳ ✳ ✳ ✳

'Rome wasn't built in a day. But neither was it built by lots of people throwing together a few odd surplus stones just when they felt like it. It happened because somebody had a plan and knew where to find the resources to achieve it.'

✳ ✳ ✳ ✳ ✳ ✳

'It is always easier to talk, to show sympathy and even to part with a few crusts than it is to engage in solid work and sacrifice.'

THE CUTTING EDGE

Lotu Pasifika Productions started life as the production unit of the Pacific Conference of Churches and became independent in the early 1980s when Seru Verabalavu, a school teacher, succeeded in building a self-sufficient publishing house.

Recognizing the difficulties of trying to publish and distribute over all the Pacific islands, LPP concentrated sales and distribution on two bookshops and a van which regularly did a three-week tour of the islands in and around Fiji, making extensive use of the ferries.

LPP produced books for schools on behalf of the Ministry of Education, pioneered Ladybird Books in the Pacific by taking subsidized colour sheets from the UK and supplying their own texts, and became distributors for a series of children's books from Japan.

They also ran an annual creative writing competition with a prize of F$600 which was promoted on Radio Fiji three times a day for two months and gave them considerable publicity and anything up to 500 entries.

Increased initiative and activity showed itself in the growth of their list, which by 1990 ran to 40 titles (25 in Fijian, 10 in English and 5 other), and also in their sales figures, which rose rapidly. By the end of the decade they were showing a small operating profit for the first time and in the early 1990s were able to acquire new headquarters.

Recently they changed their name from Lotu Pasifica Productions to Sunrise Publishers because 'Lotu' in Fijian means 'church' and has caused confusion in some people's minds with the arrival of strange sects.

THE CHANGING FACE

The Asia Theological Seminary (ATS) in Manila, in the Philippines, was founded by American missionaries. It has a library of 15,000 titles, a one-year lay-training course, an extension course and a three year post-collegiate Doctor of Ministry. Two-thirds of the staff are expatriates. Good lines of communication back to base means they are not significantly short of funds, but strong missionary roots are not always conducive to local needs. Sometimes a partnership can help.

Penuel College, in Quezon City, is 'their baby', born in 1984, the brainchild of younger Filipino staff at ATS who felt the need for something more in the nature of a Bible school for local people.

Classes are in Tagalog and English with an emphasis on raising the standards of leadership in the churches in some of the poorest parts of the country. Currently they offer a Certificate in Holistic Ministry, a Diploma and a Bachelor's degree in Theology and have around 100 students.

Many of the teachers come at their own expense from ATS. The library is about one-tenth that of ATS, but the faculty are in no doubt what they want to do. They want to break away from the conservatism within many of the mainstream churches and provide a theological education more related to social action, social need and the local situation.

Blood Brothers

Imagine two people: one lives in a home and has a job, the other lives on the streets or in the fields and has nothing. Reflect on what might happen if, just for once, the first really entered into the experience of the second. Could he ever go back by the same way?

If it is not possible to see Willy Russell's *Blood Brothers*, a reading of the play should help.

Put Hassan Dehqani-Tafti's experience side by side with that of the Wise Men (Matthew 2: 1-11).

— both travelled into someone else's world instead of staying in their own world as spectators.

— neither knew where they were going, when or whether they would arrive, and what it would look like if they did.

— both had to discover what it meant to straggle two cultures — two faiths — in order to enter the world of 'the other'.

— both had to leave a life of relative security and luxury and enter the world of the poor.

— both, when they thought they had 'arrived', quickly found themselves on the road again (in Hassan's case in exile) and in a different direction from the one they expected.

— both, ever afterwards, had to live with the tension in 'the world of the other'. Not everybody thought such attention to 'the baby' (the poor) was a good idea!

T. S. Eliot's poem, 'Journey of the Magi', is a familiar Christmas reading and may extend the imagination further. Note especially the lines,

'Then at dawn we came down to
    a temperate valley,
Wet, below the snowline . . .
But there was no information, so we
continued . . .'

Reflect on their feelings, indeed their hopes, of having arrived. It was warm after the cold of the mountains. This must surely be 'it'. But it wasn't. Why? Because 'there was no information'. So they went on. When you don't know just what you are looking for you must keep going until you find it.

These Wise Men set out looking for birth, and they found it, but it was a birth which for them turned out to be death — death to the old. Once they had tasted the new they could no longer be content with the old — no longer could they live happily in the old kingdoms (or territory), no more could they accept the old dispensation. But the experience was such that they had no doubts they would be 'glad of another death'.

Is that what happens to everyone who enters into the feelings of the poor and the needy? And if it happened to us, would we regard it as the sort of death we would welcome? And might we say afterwards that that death was the best Christmas present we ever had?

Travelling Out

Where are we to focus attention in order to appreciate the Christmas message?

1 The church, with its regular run of Christmas festivities? Are we lighting the right candle? Are the hymns PC? And 'don't you dare listen to that bishop who suggested Mary may not have been a virgin!'

2 An extravagant outpouring of love, concern and generosity? Gifts for the Christchild? And 'don't you dare revive the ghost of Ebenezer Scrooge! '

3 In the family? Isn't it nice to be with your own? But then, which 'own'? The 2.4? The church? The world Christian community? And 'don't you dare mention the multi-faith, multi-cultural world or the pluralistic family!'

Distinguish 'travelling in' (everybody going back to their place of origin) and 'travelling out'.

'The word became flesh . . . ' (John 1: 14). Incarnation is identification. Not God turning in on himself, but God 'travelling out' to identify with us, so that we (through our travelling) may better identify with others. From there we may work out fresh ways to prepare for Christmas and give expression to it.

Developing nations are not looking to us for Christmas generosity, nor even expecting that after Christmas we may see them differently. They would prefer some evidence that we have begun to feel our oneness with them as God demonstrated his oneness with us — some fresh indication that we can the better appreciate *their* feelings and enter into *their* way of life.

Even the thought can be scarey. We fear change and what it might do to us. Loss of tradition, culture, sovereignty, a way of life — convictions even. *We* may become like *them*. We may get lost in inter-faith activities, pluralism and multiculturalism. But why are we so sure *our* convictions are the *only* ones, or even the *right* ones?

Perhaps people always do. The Israelites were afraid of it when they entered Canaan, Jews when they met Gentile Christianity, Christians when they encountered Greeks and Romans, Catholics when they met Protestants. Yet so much of what we now treasure is the product of those ever-widening circles and deepening of our understanding.

Christmas could be God's invitation to us to identify in new ways with the Third World, the struggling nations and the developing countries, their poverty, their way of life, their faith, their trading patterns and the challenge and opportunities for love created by travel, the global village and immigration.

Fears and dangers there will be on the way. The good — even the Perfect — may be lost, killed, crucified. The gaps between us are so wide and some are wider than others. But no gap between humans can be greater than that between humans and God, and God bridged that one.

CARIBBEAN SPEAKS OUT

'True mission is not dropping in on Haiti — as one missionary group did — setting up a **private swimming pool,** and then offering poor people five dollars for every person they persuaded to be baptized.

True mission is a presentation of the wholeness of God's good news. No substitutes will do.'

✳ ✳ ✳ ✳ ✳ ✳ ✳

'Our chief need today is not for missionaries. In many cases it isn't even for money. It is for **partnership** — the recognition that we belong to each other and that we can learn from each other.'

✳ ✳ ✳ ✳ ✳ ✳ ✳

'Thinking globally means trying to see the consequences of your actions from the viewpoint of **those on the receiving end.**

Those on the receiving end have every right to be deeply critical of those modern missionaries who arrive in their wide-bodied jets and then proceed to proclaim their message without reference to the local church and the work going on.'

*Dr **Alan Kirton**, General Secretary of the Conference of Caribbean Churches, in London, addressing nearly 200 representatives from Catholic and Protestant missionary societies who were looking for ways in which British churches could 'think global' and 'act local', September 1986.*

Things to Do

Begin with Alan Kirton's plea, 'Real Mission', reflect on 'A Two-Tier System' and then work out a programme to educate British churchgoers to the damaging effects of world tourism and suggest ways in ways travel could be more positive.

Here are some suggestions to start you off. See what works and then construct a simple programme of education which you could commend to others.

1 Collect a random batch of tourist brochures and make a picture of what they offer so as to see ourselves. Who do the tourist operators think we are? What do they think we want? What do they think they are selling us?

2 Next time you have a speaker from a missionary society or aid agency talking about their travels and experiences overseas, ask yourself the same questions.

3 If you can persuade others in your circle to do the same meet, and talk about it.

4 Arrange a discussion group for people who have visited Third World countries on holiday to relate their experiences and show their slides. What did they see? What did they feel? What did they learn? What did they miss?

5 Read 'When the Tourists Flew In' and discuss Ten Commandments for Tourists.

6 When people who have travelled come back with their latest 'need', look critically and carefully at what you are being asked to do. Is it really the best way of helping or is it more a way of relieving somebody's guilt? It may be more honest (and 'healing') to pursue the request with questions and evaluation and come to a sound judgment than simply to 'be nice' and offer some loose change.

REAL MISSION!

'Two world conferences on Third World tourism both came to the conclusion that in its present form it is to **the disadvantage** of Third World countries. Even before tourism took off in the Caribbean, only 44 cents of every dollar stayed in the country. Now, with mass tourism, it is a lot less.'

So says Alan Kirton, General Secretary of the Conference of Caribbean Churches, pleading with churches in Britain to educate their congregations to the damaging effects of world tourism and to develop other ways in which travel and tourism could be used as a positive Christian force.'That really would be mission!' he declared.

A TWO-TIER SYSTEM

Duty Free Shops have increasingly become a feature of life in the Third World and Eastern Europe over the last 10-15 years. They are naturally popular with expatriates and tourists.

Quality goods and luxury goods, drink and tobacco, not normally available duty free except at the airports, can now be purchased in the High Street provided you have the foreign currency or the credit card. And who can blame those who take advantage of them?

Yet they are one more extension of an ever-encroaching two-tier system, and when we use them it is worth pausing to imagine how it feels for those who will never be able to take advantage of them.

Or think of a man leaving a Third World country and going to buy a snack in the departure lounge. 'Foreign currency only', says the assistant. Fine if he is a foreigner and has some foreign currency in his pocket. Not so fine if he is a national and has not yet had a chance to get some.

Food for Thought
— Food for Prayer

For Confession

A great capacity for looking — and a poor capacity for seeing.

A tendency to rush in with help and solutions before we have begun to understand the problem.

A failure to question schemes which look good on the surface but have flaws on further examination.

A weakness for seeing things from our point of view and failing to appreciate how different they look to others.

For Others

For local people in tourist spots who have had so much taken from them and yet are required to give so much to their visitors.

For the people of Iran — and many others like them — who live on the frontiers of two or more cultures or religions and have to live with the conflict.

For those who in that situation exercise a ministry of teaching theology or producing books to help people to appreciate their social situation or to change it.

RUSSIAN JOURNALIST

Give thanks for a minister and journalist, based in Moscow, and Editor-in-Chief of a monthly Baptist newspaper, in colour.

— for regular devotional material for ministers, articles for the elderly and pages for children. 'There is almost no Christian literature for teaching children in our country', he says.

— for the way he copes with limited tools. 'Computer? Fax? Phone? My only tools are a pen and a notebook.'

Pray

— for solid, long-term help rather than occasional gifts. 'Crusts are not the answer', he says, though he might not say no to a few crusts if they happened to be a few kilos of ink or a few tonnes of paper!

— for his family and for the demands made upon him by the churches for pastoral work. 'Twenty-four hours in a day is not enough for me', he says.

Pray for Editors

in their constant search for good manuscripts and new writers,

and for Writers' Workshops where writers can find encouragement and learn their craft

LENT
A Time to Question

Theme

So the last will be first, and the first will be last.

Matthew 20: 16 (NRSV)

In English, 'Lent' means 'spring'. It comes from a time when there was no Good Friday and was an anticipation of the resurrection. Not a time to be sad and live in darkness — more a time to celebrate the coming of the light, though not without an awareness of the price of suffering that stood between them. Pascha and resurrection were one. The time for preparing candidates for confirmation. Choices were being made.

The pain of Lent is not of the self-imposed variety which too often turns us in on ourselves. It is rather the sufferings of Jesus to bring light in the darkness as revealed in our contemporaries. Through their sufferings we enter into the heart and mind of Jesus, and vice versa.

So how come these quite unnecessary sufferings were ever inflicted in the first place? How come so many people failed to appreciate what this well-intentioned human being was trying to do? How come so many forces combined to bring him to such a cruel end? What on earth did he want them to do? And why were they so resistant?

But then in the sufferings of our contemporaries we begin to see how the story of the crowds in the New Testament is our story. Through the Looking Glass we see ourselves and the role we play in inflicting suffering and judgment on others.

These sufferings are not exactly self-inflicted, accidental or plain unlucky. They have a cause. And we may be part of it, either by our actions or by our policies. Read Isaiah 53: 2-7 and imagine the Suffering Servant to be the developing nations. For 'he' read 'they'. Hebrew distinctions between the one and the many are imprecise and some scholars have long identified the Suffering Servant with a nation rather than an individual. Are they wounded for our transgressions, crushed for our iniquities? Is the punishment that made us whole imposed on them, and are we healed by their bruises?

Slowly we begin to see the choice in front of us.

key word	Lent is the time to make a choice — to choose positively to identify with the sufferings of others knowing that if we fail to share in their sufferings we may not be able to share in their resurrection. This is different from self-imposed discipline to achieve holiness and the discovery itself can be painful. But then to choose a different way of life is more painful.
Choice	

The New Professionalism

If you doubt the capacity of the mirror to challenge the way you normally look at things try cutting your hair through one. Without a lot of practice the scissors nearly always go the wrong way. That's why, when it comes to aid, there is a lot to be said for seeing it through the looking glass. It reverses our impressions and images. It challenges our prejudices and it brings out some of the ways we inflict unnecessary suffering on others.

Take, for example, the popular notion that what the Third World needs more than money is education. True or false? Before you answer, try another question. If you were about to say 'education' where did you assume the education would come from? Us? Of course, because we have the knowledge and the expertise and we are the professionals.

But what about *their* knowledge — the knowledge they already have? There is fair evidence that in many respects, notably agriculture, their knowledge as local people is far superior to that of aid workers and Western specialists going in, but who ever stops to listen? As a result much local knowledge is wasted and Western specialists deprive themselves of a glorious opportunity to learn something which may be to their advantage.

But what hurts most is that such behaviour utterly and entirely demolishes any confidence which those people had in themselves. That suffering is unnecessary. To appreciate it we have to see it from their point of view.

Alongside this idea goes the equally fallacious notion that they are incapable. They may *know*, but they can't *achieve*! But which of *us* has ever tried to achieve anything in *their* circumstances? Many Westerners have sat and watched people in the Third World, both at work and at play, and seen that they have 'secrets' which the West has never found. Many have come away wondering whether they, their friends and acquaintances could ever survive so long, in such conditions, and with so little. To begin to feel their hurt is to begin also to feel we ought perhaps to do something about it.

Robert Chambers says one way of responding might be to aim at a new professionalism using a different language. He makes lists of words. Power, comfort, wealth, things, clean, tidy, controlled and certainty are all First World words. Weakness, discomfort, poverty, people, dirty, untidy, uncontrolled and doubt are Third World words. What are the chances we can enter into their discomfort sufficiently to use their language and run the risk of discovering how very different everything seems when we talk about it in a different way.

'Bottom-up' rather than 'Top-Down' is another way of saying the same thing. Aid workers and their associates are for ever talking about getting down to the 'grass roots' or the 'coal face'. But why 'down' unless we want to stress the point that we are starting from the top? Which of course many aid programmes are. They start in London or New York, Geneva or Bonn, and then they are offered in a paternalistic way to those who can do little other than accept. But supposing the schemes were to start at the grass roots or the coal face and then work their way down to the bottom of the pit where the gold reserves are always kept? We might begin to see wealth in a different light.

From there we might glimpse the new professionalism which Chambers is often writing about. Normal professionalism, he says, exists for the people who belong to it. Indeed the creation of a specialist 'club' or 'inner circle' is what normal professionalism is about. It is for those who have achieved a certain standard, laid down and examined by those who are there already. Others cannot expect to be admitted lightly and it is a way of preserving standards for those who have succeeded.

The customers (or clients) will always come second because what the customer wants may not always be in the best interests of the profession. Convenient consulting hours for a doctor are not necessarily the same thing as convenient consulting hours for his patients. Banking hours certainly weren't, though they have changed for the better in recent years! And even in church circles it is well known that it is extraordinarily difficult to change something or to introduce something new if the local incumbent, priest or minister is not in favour of it.

Similarly, a new professionalism for the Third World means learning to see everything from the opposite point of view to such an extent that each project, programme and design begins, develops and ends in the Third World, the West supplying only such finance and know-how as is necessary. And when both sides are stuck then that is the moment for the two to sit down on the same height of chair and work out the solution together.

That is real aid. That is education. And the identification which began in Advent and Christmas finds fulfilment in choosing to share in the sufferings throughout the season of Lent. [3.1]

'If the present growth rates were to double, only seven poor countries would reach the level of the rich majority in 100 years and only nine would do so in the next 1000 years. In the meantime all the gains of "growth" go to the few; one-fifth of the world consumes four-fifths of its resources, while child malnutrition increases, with 43,000 deaths every day. The majority cannot feed themselves often because they are compelled by their foreign creditors to grow luxury crops for the rich — such as coffee and carnations. This is the real meaning of "international market forces at work" and the unspoken price of "growth". It is a truth that ought to be printed as a health warning in the financial sections of newspapers.' [3.2]

Famines do not occur — they are organized by the grain trade (Brecht)

LISTENING TO THE LOCAL PEOPLE

THE WOMEN

'Women in developing countries do face special problems, but they have shown that they have the ability, the enthusiasm and the will to work for real improvements in their daily lives. Our task is to help them.'

. . . .

'A few years ago, relatively few development programmes considered the different roles of men and women. Water pumps were being installed without asking women — the main users — where they wanted them. Literacy projects were set up for women without creches or usable seats for their children. Training in new agricultural methods was offered only to men, even when women made many of the decisions on the farm and did most of the work in the field.

Changes started after the United Nations Decade for Women from 1975 to 1985 . . . (and) . . . the shift in thinking has produced some surprising benefits. On a bridge-building project in Cameroon — following consultation with the local women — the engineers designed access points so that women could carry on washing their clothes in the local river.' [3.3]

THE PEACEMAKERS

Robert Archer, writing about Conflict and Peacemaking in the Southern Sudan, describes traditional ways of handling conflict compared to methods employed within the peace and justice programme of the New Sudan Council of Churches, based on techniques of conflict resolution developed abroad, mainly in the United States. He says,

'My own view is that the traditional mechanisms for resolving conflict at local level are potentially very powerful and effective, because Sudanese consider them legitimate and know how to use them. Their use empowers the local community and works to its strengths. Both these features are important.

By contrast, I see four serious drawbacks to any programme that relies heavily on overseas observers or on conflict-resolution techniques that are foreign.

1 The Sudanese already have had too many experiences of dependency.

2 Traditional methods are very effective.

3 Too many overseas monitors would be needed.

4 Monitors could easily become targets.' [3.4]

THE RURAL FARMERS

The links of modern, scientific knowledge with wealth, power and prestige condition outsiders to despise and ignore rural people's own knowledge. Priorities in crop, livestock and forestry research reflect biases against what matters to rural people. Rural people's knowledge is often superior to that of outsiders. . . Rural people's knowledge and modern scientific knowledge are complementary in their strengths and weaknesses. Combined they may achieve what neither would alone. For such combinations outsider professionals have to step down off their pedestals, and sit down, listen and learn. [3.5]

VICTIMS AND CARERS

In situations of crisis and disaster we mostly do not have any choice whether we are victims or carers for victims. Much depends on where we are born and what happens. The line between the two is often very narrow. Nor is it always fixed. A carer today may be a victim tomorrow and vice versa.

Where we do have a choice is whether we want to identify with the victims and care for them or whether we find it more convenient 'to pass by on the other side'.

One way of addressing these issues is to look at both, preferably in a mirror, so that we see ourselves as part of the picture. We may then find that we ask a different set of questions and come up with a different set of answers.

Recent events in South America may help. In a situation of crisis and disaster, they demonstrate how local people addressed their own problems and responded to the calls made on them by their own people. They also show how literature plays an important part in a wider social programme of care, in one case leading to its production and in the other as a vehicle for expressions of protest and concern.

CRISIS AND DISASTER

Human catastrophe can happen anywhere and to anybody, but it is always worst when it strikes the poor or those who are 'down already'. It comes in many shapes and sizes — earthquakes, floods, volcanic eruptions, hurricanes, temporary famine and permanent hunger — and creates as many problems, reactions and opportunities as there are people involved. No two disasters, no two victims, are exactly the same.

But whatever it is, whether in extremely difficult terrain or in some remote corner of the world, scarcely has it happened than volunteers and rescue teams, often in their hundreds, are on the scene. The desire to rescue people in distress seems to be universal.

Not surprisingly, initially at least, there will be a preoccupation with the number of victims, the extent of the loss in financial terms, replacement costs and so on.

Only recently has much thought been given to the emotional effects on the survivors, and especially to the more personal and long-term effects of crisis trauma. But things are changing. Help no longer ceases at the point of rescue, after which the sufferers will be expected to manage on their own.

Less than a decade ago books and articles on the subject were few and far between. They are still not all that numerous though they are increasing, which makes the response of the churches of Latin America at that time all the more laudable.

Two organizations, the Latin American Council of Churches (CLAI) and EIRENE (a Churches' Family Pastoral Counselling organization), both with headquarters in Ecuador, took the initiative.

The starting point was the volcanic eruption in Colombia in 1985, when CLAI and EIRENE brought together a group of Christian specialists in Ecuador to train professionals (nurses, social workers, Red Cross, civil servants and volunteers) to handle the emotional problems of the victims.

Following this crisis they produced four booklets:

— a basic instruction booklet on handling crisis

— a less technical booklet on recovering from tragedy

— a work book to help families cope with emotional crises

— a work book for children, arising out of the realization that since children tend to recover more quickly than adults they can often exercise a ministry of their own by helping parents and friends.

The next impetus came from the 1987 earthquake in Ecuador, when these booklets, adapted and amplified, were used as the basis for a three-day workshop for more than 500 doctors, nurses, social workers, psychiatrists, psychologists, etc. Members were grouped in batches of 30, dealing with such topics as handling an emergency and long-term preventative work. Over 10,000 copies were distributed, some paid for by local churches.

In September 1987 they had requests from churches in Venezuela and one doctor gave a week of his own time to assist in the counselling programme. In November they helped to train workers with radio-active victims in Brazil. In January 1988 they trained rescue workers after the floods in Rio de Janiero and in January 1989, following the hurricane, they worked in Nicaragua, by which time it was realized that the information gleaned and the experience gained had relevance also to war victims, refugees, widows, orphans, exiles, the unemployed, displaced persons and the families of those who had 'disappeared'.

To begin with they certainly did not find it an easy subject to handle. If a catastrophe leads to a shortage of food, for example, it is not too difficult to work out how much food you need, how many aeroplanes to fly in the resources, how many trucks,

what distances they have to travel, what it will cost, etc. In ways like this those who remain can tackle the problem of rebuilding the nation or the community. What CLAI and EIRENE wanted to tackle was the rebuilding of the individuals in their emotional crisis.

Their strength was that they did not allow themselves personally to get involved in the crisis work. Instead, they concentrated on the training of others and the preparation of appropriate literature. Their reward came as their work received increasing recognition. Their book on handling crisis, for example, was widely in demand in Latin America, with further requests from the Caribbean Council of Churches and for translations into English and other languages from The Councils of Churches for Asia and Africa.

Their insights serve two purposes. They enable those who so far have not encountered such tragedy to enter into the experience of those who have, to feel at one with them in the work they are doing and so enter into a relationship with them through prayer and worship. They also enable others to learn from them and so make a more effective contribution when confronted with similar, if more ordinary and less extreme, situations.

The story further illustrates the initiatives and creativity of many Christian people in developing countries, their ability to assess and tackle their own problems, their capacity to raise at least some of their own funds, and their skill in making a literary and educational contribution to the wider church and world.

Theologically, the story is full of positives emerging from a no-hope situation. It demonstrates what can happen when people are at their lowest ebb, like the victims of natural catastrophe and disaster or like the disciples on the resurrection morning, provided there is someone on hand to give hope and support. Life can be found, even in a grave.

DANGER AND OPPORTUNITY

Some 'crisis' insights from Christian literature in South America may help us not only to understand them but to understand ourselves as well

They begin with the Chinese word for crisis, made up of two other words, one meaning 'danger' and the other 'opportunity'. 'Any crisis,' they say, 'is a combination of two realities: a danger and an opportunity.' So how do we respond positively to catastrophe?

Learn to Recognize Symptoms

Incredulity. 'It can't really have happened!'

Inability to sleep

Feelings of irritability, anxiety or depression

Physical effects, such as headache or diarrhoea

Anger and self-recrimination

Making unreasonable demands. 'Somebody (the government?) must do something to give me back what I have lost.'

Blocking out the memory

Over activity, including work or travel

Extreme passivity

Suicide

Until we bring such symptoms out into the open 'opportunity' is prevented from surfacing, though often reactions may not surface immediately and sometimes can take a very long time.

Steps to Caring

Caring begins by sharing with the victims in the process of emotional recuperation

Listening with care, attention and concern

Encouraging sufferers to talk about what happened

Reflection

Finding ways of expressing grief

Helping people to accept loss

Recognizing the good intentions in the way they behave

Stimulating victims (and their families) to join actively in community projects

Confronting the question of suicide

Communicating faith and hope

Giving special attention to children

Fifty Lessons

Christians in South America have produced a practical work book, dealing with survival, recuperation and growth (or initial help, long term treatment, and convalescence) setting out fifty lessons, each of which is followed by a space for people to write down (or draw) some of their own reactions and observations. For example,

the five losses which they regard as the most serious

what actually happened to them personally when it all began

what they feel now.

Children are introduced to fifteen lessons as steps on a staircase — take them one at a time!

CHOICES FOR WOMEN

In many places the choices are few — choosing your response is paramount

DEPENDENCY

In Zimbabwe the Association of Women's Clubs has over 100 clubs with a membership of 23,000, mostly in rural areas. They were started by the white women in the early 1950s and only 'went black' after independence when most of the white women withdrew.

Without that white support they depend entirely on outside funding agencies, mostly in Scandinavia and the Netherlands, and know only too well that their programme is dictated by what the outside funding agencies are prepared to pay for.

One of their major needs, for example, is buildings and salaries. The funding agencies are not interested. One responded by saying they were only interested in food processing, which was of no value whatsoever. Their members produce a list of needs in order of priority but the clubs know they have no way of meeting them unless the donors also want them.

They are struggling to establish a reference library of titles relating to their field of interest in their headquarters, but their only hope is to find a donor who happens to be interested in reading.

'This makes it very difficult to feel that the work is ours', they say. 'Before independence we knew we were dependent on the "white women". Now we have a dependence of a different sort.'

VIOLATION

Women in Costa Rica are marginalized, not only in society but also in the church.

Strong, male-dominated Catholicism in the country as a whole has not helped. The loss of virginity was a sin, but only because it was an offence against a man who had been led into immorality, and if a girl from the country became pregnant by her landlord her chief offence was what she had done to him!

Education over recent years has achieved something. Women have started to ask questions. They even sense the liberating power of the gospel. But not much else. In some respects in Central America the lot of women has got worse.

In Guatemala, for example, many have been widowed by civil strife. In Nicaragua, husbands and sons are away fighting. Many live in constant fear or anxiety because their men folk have been, or are, in danger of being 'disappeared'.

So they carry enormous burdens of violation running homes, caring for children and working for a living, yet knowing that their hopes for a better lot depend on men and women working together as equals.

Feminism here is fighting for the rights which women in Europe and North America have taken for granted for half a century.

CULTURE

In the Caribbean what they are trying to discover is the role of women *in the Caribbean* for today. Their problem is that over the years they have been the victims of so many conflicting forces.

Traditionally, the Caribbean woman was wife, mother, housekeeper, worker and breadwinner, local politician and social servant. For many it meant an involvement in civic affairs. They had a clear understanding of who they were, where they were, and why they were there.

Then came the British. The cultures intermingled and the role of the ideal woman was narrowed to that of wife and mother.

More recently the harsher strains of North American feminism came in over the air waves and the role is beginning to change again.

The Caribbean woman though is made of sterner stuff than to allow herself to be buffeted by the latest fashion.

For her, the first issue is not 'women' but 'Caribbean life and culture'. It is to discover the role of women which will be most helpful to that end.

MARRIAGE — TIE OR LIBERATION?

Can the developing nations help us to a further 'face' of feminism — transcending sexist language, a female Holy Spirit and the motherhood of God to a richer awareness of what it means to be a person?

Vera Brittain relates how, during and after the First World War, she was struggling with the problems of feminism, and wondering whether it was possible for a woman to marry and have children and yet continue with her own career and maintain her intellectual and spiritual independence.

She and her fiancé decided it was, provided their marriage was always subservient to their work. Marriage must not be an end in itself. It must be a liberating force enabling each partner to be most truly themselves. [3.6]

Perhaps their experience can help us to a better understanding of the familiar lines of Kahlil Gibran.

Love one another, but make not a bond of love:
Let it rather be a moving sea between the shores of your souls.

Fill each other's cup but drink not from one cup,
Give one another of your bread but eat not from the same loaf.

Sing and dance together and be joyous, but let each one of you be alone,
Even as the strings of a lute are alone though they quiver with the same music.

Give your hearts, but not into each other's keeping,
For only the hand of Life can contain your hearts.

And stand together yet not too near together:
For the pillars of the temple stand apart,
And the oak tree and the cypress grow not in each other's shadow. [3.7]

CHOICES FOR WIDOWS

Ariel Dorfman's 'Widows' choose to keep up the struggle

Dorfman's *Widows* is about the horrors of too many women in Chile in the early 1970s whose menfolk had 'been disappeared', and about the choice between accepting it and coming to terms with it or continuing to hope and fighting the authorities that brought it about.

But what happened there can happen anywhere — 'where a few men decide the life and death of the rest of the people . . . that one man shall "disappear" . . . that another man shall go into exile and never see his children again'.

Nor is it only yesterday, or in Chile, that people live in a world where justice too often goes wrong. We all do — and all the time. 'Mistakes' kill. Governments act behind closed doors.

People are repeatedly told to keep their head down, to come to terms with what is happening, to see it is for the best, and not to confront the issue. There is nothing they can do. Life must go on.

And so it is in *Widows*. Violence marches on until Alexandra, a widow who has been the chief proponent of that philosophy, has a change of heart:

> 'When they took Emiliano away,' she says, 'I thought if I keep quiet and still they won't hurt him and he'll come back, someday, safe. They made me dance their steps every day, ever since. Quiet and still, we all thought that, but there's always someone else they can take.'

The same sentiment is expressed by another widow who says, thoughtfully and quietly, 'In a way, I feel responsible'.

It is the grandmother who refuses to let go. She pleads with her family to keep up the struggle. She is an inactive activist, a consuming irritation to those who know how to handle the violent but have no defence against the passive resister.

In the end she probably pays the ultimate sacrifice, but not before a final showdown with the army Captain, who, with the power and the guns, reminds her that if only she would surrender and co-operate he could save her and all her family. And the old woman promptly reminds him, both by word and deed, where true power lies.

Widows is never likely to be a popular play. It is too much about the choice between staying with the familiar, the convenient and the comfortable or probing the uncomfortable, but as the author said in Cambridge after the European première,

> 'There has to be a place, if only a small one, for a play like this. We live in a world where the whole message of the media is for something light, something soothing, something comforting, and nothing to disturb or disrupt. Yet violence — institutional violence — is everywhere. And the message of this whole play is that violence solves nothing.'

THE CUTTING EDGE

EIRENE (Centro de la Familia) is an interdenominational pastoral association, based in Ecuador and working in five other countries in South America.

Its object is to create peace (*eirene*) in the family — not to sort out quarrels or disagreements, but to create an atmosphere where either they don't break out or they can be handled satisfactorily.

This requires the training of professional counsellors in family therapy with an emphasis on crisis intervention who see the family as a whole. 'The person alleged to be the problem within a family is not necessarily the source of the difficulty — often it is the weakest member of the family who has fallen a prey to all the forces reacting on them.' Counselling therefore is for the whole family and not just 'the problem member'.

It also calls for close links with pastors, lay workers and professionals in other disciplines, for workshops and, of course, publishing.

EIRENE has produced three training manuals for professional workers, each about 250 A4 pages plus six cassettes. The first was *Marriage Enrichment for Couples,* the second dealt with teenage relationships, covering topics such as identity, sexuality and premarital planning, and the third was on family integration, seeing the family as part of the community and so enabling them to move into the notion of God's family.

Many copies were handed out free to those most in need, sold at a discount to poor groups, and cost $50 to those who could afford them. Requests came from churches, seminaries, universities, professional and lay, both inside and outside Ecuador, but none of it would have been possible without subsidy.

EIRENE also produced a series of probing monographs and an annotated booklist twice a year for professional people, and became involved with the Council of Churches for Latin America in a programme of crisis and disaster counselling.

THE CHANGING FACE

Taiwan Theological College and Seminary, founded by a Canadian missionary in 1872, is one of four theological schools of the Presbyterian Church in Taiwan.

There are over 60 MDiv students, men outnumbering women three to one, but of the 140 studying Christian Education, Music, and Church and Society the proportions are reversed.

The library has over 30,000 volumes, 22,000 in English and other Western languages, 8,000 in Chinese and 800 in other languages.

In a country where only 2-3% of the population are Christian, folk religion and Asian (especially Chinese) music and musical instruments receive attention, and the College is looking at ways in which the Reformed Tradition can be fitted into an Asian context.

Women's issues surface at three points: among future ministers' wives, on topics of special concern (such as home and family) and on more radical feminist questions. Relationships with Episcopal, Mennonite and Methodist churches are constantly being encouraged.

NO ROOM

A Reflection
for two readers on Mark 2: 1-12

What a good thing we got here on time. Seems we're too late. We can't get in.

Quiet, please. We're trying to hear the sermon.

Make way, please. Make way for the disabled.

No room. No room. Clear off!

We'll have to come back tomorrow — but perhaps tomorrow is going to be too late.

Good. Perhaps we can have some peace now.

There must be another way of doing things.

There's a time and a place for everything.

This sort of thing can't be right. Keeping the handicapped out can't be right.

This sort of thing can't be right. Interrupting the sermon can't be right.

Let's do something about it. Things can't go on like this.

We must stand up for what is proper. Things can't go on like this.

If at first we don't succeed, then we have to try to find another way.

People should follow the proper procedures.

Unless we take some risk, we'll never get anywhere.

I don't like it. It will lead to the breakdown of all authority.

Right, let's get on with it. Give us that chopper.

[3.8]

The Crowd and the Paralytic

Begin with the paralytic (Mark 2: 1-12). Of all those present he most of all wants to exercise the privilege of choice. And he knows exactly what he wants to choose; to be accepted and able to live like other people.

Identify him in today's world. He is everywhere, from friends with a chip on their shoulder to minority groups, to pressure groups and victims of pressure groups, to sections of society which are suspect because of their race, culture, orientation, family connections, etc, and even to whole nations who feel consigned for ever to sit round a table where the best things of life are never for them.

Ask next why they can't have it. In this story the answer is very clear. They can. They are entitled to it as much as the next person, and the means of giving it to them are on hand. The only trouble is the crowd that gets in the way.

So the next thing to do is to identify the crowd. Who are these 'nasty people' who prevent this man from having a fuller life? Avoid going for leaders such as dictators, bishops or politicians. They are few in number and any power they have is only because the crowd affords it to them. Avoid seeing the crowd as 'nasty'. Before we have finished we might even see ourselves there 'in the mirror'.

This crowd is a mixture of other people with similar needs, people who enjoy a spectacle, people indulging their own appetite, people so preoccupied with themselves that they are totally insensitive to the paralytic, and a group who are there for the sole purpose of preventing anything happening and 'knocking it' as soon as it does.

Some of them are certainly in the church. Many more are outside. They don't *all* get in the way *all* the time, but they are all liable to get in the way some of the time.

Some are too preoccupied with their own concerns and viewpoint even to notice the basic needs around them. Some are pre-conditioned to oppose what they don't personally like, and in extreme cases actually use their 'commitment to Jesus' to prevent others finding fulfilment through him. They join pressure groups, resist change, write letters to the press and 'campaign against'.

Eventually frustration leads to violence because the few who really care find that the only thing they can do is to abandon the normal route and tear up the roof. Prophecy is self-fulfilling. 'We always knew they were like that!' But did we ever see what made them like that?

Only Jesus seems to see 'the violence' as an expression of faith (v 5). What makes fullness of life possible is not so much the determination of 'the man', for he was too helpless, but the faith of 'the four'. It was their choice that made the difference. If they could accept him Jesus could accept him too. Once the man was convinced about the love (and forgiveness) of his friends it was but a small step to feel the love of Jesus. And when Jesus says, 'Your sins are forgiven', what he is doing is to assert his right to a full life.

Invite people to nominate those in today's world who would welcome this kind of choice and the idea of Changing Things for Good, including the disabled, the developing nations and the poor in our own country (see below p. 46.). Can we (dare we?) nominate others who would oppose them?

Read Mark 2: 1-12 in the King James Version, then read No Room (page 44) with a tiny minority (certainly not more than four) reading the italics and as many as possible reading the rest, the minority whispering and anxious, the majority confident, noisy and ebullient.

Finally, re-read the parable in a soft voice or invite everyone to read it aloud but only in a whisper, and in a modern version.

Bent Double — and No Stars!

Imagine the life and the personal problems of this woman who was bent double and could not stand up straight (Luke 13: 10-17).

Long before it was fashionable to talk about 'a new professionalism' or viewing the world 'bottom-up' this woman had a totally different perspective from her contemporaries. Imagine how different our world would be if we saw it as she did.

Did she ever roll herself on her back, in the open on a dark night, to see the stars? Identify individuals and groups in society, especially in the developing world, who surely feel as she did.

Guttierez says the Hebrew word *ani* (one of the most commonly used in the Old Testament for the poor) has multiple meanings, but one of them is 'the bent-over one, the one labouring under a load, the one not in possession of full health and vigour'.

In the Old Testament these are the people for whom reapers had to leave the corners of the field unreaped so that they could collect their share when everybody else had gone and so avoid embarrassment. Think of people today who occupy city centres when everybody else has left and collect what they can from rubbish bins. Contrast the 'stars' who walk the city streets during the day with the poor who are unable to see any stars at all.

Try to put your impression of the poor in the Third World today side by side with, say, the poor in France in the early nineteenth century as reflected in *Les Misérables* or in Britain today (see pp. 46, 106).

Make a list or collect newspaper cuttings for a week, relating to persons and groups who fit in one or more of those categories. They are the subject of our story. This woman is their patron saint.

But is there a different kind of poverty which affects the rich so that they can't see the stars either, except in terms of their pay-packets, their perks and their profits? Doctors who cannot see the stars except in terms of collaboration with a new health system which has little attraction for them? Teachers, with school assessments and inspections? Housewives and motorists, with one crazy promotion scheme after another? Is there a spiritual poverty which may afford material comfort most of the time but little else by way of satisfaction?

Perhaps this woman's story is everybody's story. Speculate on it. Was it that she couldn't see the stars because she was bent double, or was she bent double because she couldn't face the stars? Was she just reticent? Had she perhaps been told from childhood that they were not for the likes of her? Had she tried once to walk tall and got such a battering she decided never to try again? And was the pain of straightening up worth the cost of having to face up to everything around her which previously she had been able to ignore?

Insights into her story may be a key to appreciating the feelings and emotions of so many others like her. Doubtless she had been offered many cures. People down on their heels usually are. Education was probably one of them. But education for what? To believe that the stars are not for them?

Finally, do not overlook those in the story who have a vested interested in perpetuating the blindness. The Ruler of the Synagogue, who wants to create a distraction by pointing out that it is the Sabbath. Politicians, who would prefer the churches to address 'other issues'. Charities, that would prefer us to raise money rather than ask questions.

So where are we to find the miracle of healing? Perhaps in the poor themselves, as Victor Hugo suggested. From the depths of depression new life breaks out, like wheat that springs up green. Comb the papers for stories of life that rises from the ashes. This is the miracle of healing that Jesus performs. The crushed and the bent double learn to straighten up, walk tall and see stars.

This is what the poor want. Not an occasional roll on their back but a new life which lasts.

CRISIS AND DISASTER

Crisis and disaster are not confined to poorer countries. 100 unaccompanied refugee children arrive in Britain each year. One was asked what was happening in his country. 'Everyone and everything is dead', he wrote.

— some have seen their parents tortured and murdered, some have been brutally treated as a way of getting at their parents, some have been thrown against walls so as to get their mother to say where their father is and some parents know that their children are watching them being tortured.

— some arrive with their mother, their father often dead or in prison, and may spend several days in a detention centre whilst they wait to hear whether their refugee status has been accepted.

— some, brutalized by their experiences, ignorant of their rights, terrified of the consequences of asserting them, fearful of being sent back, and probably with very little English, will be looking for a school. [3.9]

Pray that those who meet them, care for them and make decisions about them may appreciate what they have suffered.

— for those with relatives to go to, those fortunate enough to be placed in the care of the local authority, and for many who will wander the streets until they are picked up.

— for schools who don't want to take them because their low attainment will lower the school in the league tables and the effect that that knowledge will have on the children.

— for those who counsel, train counsellors or produce manuals for training and guidance for victims.

Things to Do

EVALUATE A PROJECT

Take a project supported by your church, or any other charitable agency with which you are involved, and find out who are the real beneficiaries. Encourage others by starting a group or getting the subject on the agenda of a group already in existence.

1 Take a look at the regime as a whole and its politics. If its record on human rights is dubious and you cannot be absolutely sure that the help will really reach the oppressed it may be better to give nothing at all.

2 Check that any aid you give will not benefit the privileged minority. It is very difficult both to find out and to prevent.

3 Since a project to help poor people to produce more for themselves is better than gifts or direct aid, find out exactly which you are doing.

4 Examine the project in some detail:

(a) How many people will it employ?

(b) Will everyone in the community have equal access to its benefits?

(c) Who is it designed to help?

(d) What have they got already?

(e) Will the people who benefit have a say in how it is installed and run?

(f) If it is equipment or machinery, does it require power, is power available, and how reliable is it? Are there people trained to use it? What are the local facilities for maintenance and servicing?

If after all this the need is so great that you feel it would be positively immoral not to help, at least do it with your eyes open and have no illusions about what will happen to most of it.

STUDY THE RICH

'Study the rich and powerful, not the poor and powerless' (Susan George).

1 Radio and television, magazines and newspapers are very good at providing us with information about the rich and the powerful — their resources, their lives, their interests and contacts, their politics and principles, their concerns and life-styles. Soak yourselves in one or two until you feel you almost know them.

If you can draw, draw them. If you can write, draft a profile in 500 words. If you can do neither, list a dozen questions you would like to ask them and a week later try to imagine the answers.

2 Select half-a-dozen stories about the poor from similar sources and try to work out how your 'rich person' might respond to them.

3 Conduct a similar exercise with rich countries. Ignore what their leaders and politicians say. Look instead at what happens. Look at their aid and arms programmes, their overseas policies, their response to asylum seekers and ethnic minorities. Then try to see how it all looks from the point of view of a poor country or a severely disadvantaged resident.

TRICKLE DOWN?

'Nothing much trickles down from the élite, and the élite is in a position to syphon off everything that crosses its frontiers — or nearly — including charity.

Any charity ought to have as its primary goal to make itself redundant. Where social justice prevails, charity is superfluous'. [3.10]

Food for Thought
— Food for Prayer

OUR LIMITED VISION

Confess the difficulty we have in seeing things differently

— the hurt we cause and the damage we do to so many people because of our limited vision

— the way we choose to stay with the familiar, the convenient and the comfortable

— the way we so easily succumb to the feeling that 'there is nothing we can do'

— our reluctance to give to things of which we do not approve or which we cannot continue to control.

FOOD, GLORIOUS FOOD

Give thanks that not everybody in the developing world is poor or hungry. The land around the theological college at Tomahon in Sulawesi is lush. The vegetables are of a high quality — 'the best in the land and picked from the earth just up the road that very morning', they said. In neighbouring Seram the land was so fruitful that the people could find enough food from the bark of one tree to live for a month; fish they just got from the ocean. The only trouble was it produced a people who saw very little need to make much effort. Sadly, the arrival of new industries and population movements were threatening their traditional ways of life.

Category

Bible Commentaries (at different levels) for ministers, lay people, young people and new believers

Remember

Writers, broadcasters, communicators, teachers and booksellers

Focus On

something you read and have always found helpful and give thanks for the ability to read

---

VICTIMS OF TERRORISM

Pray for 50,000 people in Peru, many of them refugees, who have been scarred (emotionally, physically or both) by acts of terrorism.

— for the churches of the Andes who are reaching out to them

— for Christians working in EIRENE (Peru) who have produced and distributed booklets in Spanish and Quechua for people suffering from emotional trauma.

RAISING STANDARDS

Pray for theological colleges struggling to increase their standards so as to secure accreditation

— their shortage of cash

— their attempts to improve the library

— their desire to improve the teacher-student ratio.

Pray for Sales People and Distributors

often travelling great distances,

facing competition from bigger, secular houses, and still required to be courteous and patient.

Remember their families from whom they are separated

HOLY WEEK
A Time to Feel

Theme

My God, my God, why have you forsaken me?

Ps 22: 1; Mark 15: 34

We have made the choice. We have seen. We have heard. We have felt. The moment of commitment is approaching — to stand by our choice and be counted.

Argument about who he is and what he can do is over. By the end of Palm Sunday the die is cast. The mood is one of inevitability — there is nothing Jesus can do, nothing the crowd can do, nothing the Jewish leaders can do — each is trapped in the web they have created for themselves.

The coming week is one to eye each other, possibly to blame one another and certainly to reflect on how things might have been different. If only . . . ! But hope and the future no longer lie within their capacity to reason and argue so much as to feel — the beginnings of a paschal experience.

So what is it like to *feel* the pain of another? The pain of a mother for a sick child? Of a child, for a parent rejected by a partner or made redundant? Of a husband, for a wife unfairly treated at work? The questions alone help to explain why so often relatives are more angry and find it more difficult to cope than the sufferers themselves.

Some of it is the pain of being 'out there — with the sufferer' and yet at the same time 'isolated and unable to help'. 'Out there — with the sufferer' and yet completely misunderstood and totally unappreciated by others around who are carrying on with their daily round.

Why did Jesus have to choose the friends he did? Why did he have to die? Why couldn't he be more like you and me? And how, in the moment of deepest gloom did he feel the isolation from his Father? (Mark 15: 34).

Perhaps empathy should dominate our thinking in this season. Can we contemplate what happened to Jesus to the point of fully comprehending? Can we enter into the experience of many people who find life so extremely difficult through no fault of their own to the point where we really begin to understand? Perhaps only then will we begin to appreciate the connection between the two.

key word	*pascho* means 'to suffer or to be affected by something that befalls us', as opposed to those things that happen to us as the result of our own actions. Associated Greek words (like *pathos*) relate to anything, good or bad, that befalls us — hence the word 'sympathy', meaning that we share the same feelings, not to be confused with 'empathy', which means projecting ourselves into someone else's experience (standing in their shoes) to appreciate what they are going through.
πασχω Suffer	

Children in Need

Just when everything was building up for the excitement of Terry Wogan and the Children in Need appeal, in 1992, Bob Holman penned a thought-provoking piece, 'Children in Need of Respect', in which he raised some important questions.

Bob Holman was writing out of his experience working for the Easterhouse Project in Glasgow. They made regular applications for money from Children in Need, mainly to take deprived children on holiday. It sounds fine and anybody who doesn't get his hand down is made to feel a cad. It certainly raises a lot of money from which children suffering from cancer, arthritis, and the like stand to benefit. It's also good television. Lots of clips of children enjoying themselves on holiday. That's their way of showing that last year's money was well used and why they are entitled to ask for more this year.

But does anybody ever stop to ask what it is like for the children? 'There is something demeaning,' Holman says, 'about taking on the role of the recipient of public charity' when what we really need is not a patronizing jamboree to provide treats for people in wheel chairs but a challenge to social attitudes.

Many Third World people on the receiving end of aid in any form would echo the same idea. It is slight satisfaction to them that their stories are told repeatedly in aid literature around the world to raise money or that their photographs, often quite deliberately misrepresenting the real situation in which they live, gets splashed across the front of the religious press, the missionary society periodicals, and the aid agency journals and broad sheets, or that their countries are portrayed as dirty, backward, rural, primitive and always having disasters, when many of them live in cities not very different from those of the West and in some cases with no more social problems, though different. And they know just as well as the children of Easterhouse that what is needed is not bank loans or charitable gifts or worldwide publicity but a radical change of social and political attitudes in the countries from which the cash is coming.

But then if it is demeaning for the recipients, it is not much better for the project holders. Bob Holman knows that too because one of his jobs is to write begging letters to get the money. To succeed, he says, not only must he emphasize the weaknesses rather than the strengths of the project in which he is engaged but he must also squeeze his families into definitions of need and deprivation which will encourage the charities to respond.

Many Third World project holders who spend their time trying to secure aid would warm to that one as well. Securing aid from charitable organizations is not so much a matter of knowing what you need as of knowing what it is that the charity is likely to give, and at times that may even mean distorting what you are doing (or even what you would like to do) in order to appeal. Not for them the satisfaction of telling a good story or putting on a good show; more a matter of dwelling on what they could do, if only . . . ! It is a world in which you present your accounts to show failures rather than successes and where the reward for improvement may well mean that you get less next time round.

But the real burden of Holman's complaint is that over and above the satisfaction that comes to the giver the charity bonanzas primarily serve the interests of TV and government. It was fine for Anneka Rice to convert a disused factory into a recreation block (which Easterhouse certainly found to be an asset) but to achieve it Easterhouse was responsible for looking after eleven children who accompanied her for three days as she dashed around persuading firms to do the work, and in the end it was difficult not to feel that the children were just disposable tools, useful for bolstering the programme and at the beck and call of a TV industry marketing a personality.

Government and big business are worse. Governments much prefer the kudos which goes with handing out large sums in public to handing it out more discreetly through allowances or to ensuring that the need is not there in the first place, whilst businessmen prefer the free advertising that goes with the publicity to taxes (both personal and corporate) to ensure a different approach.

There are some aid agencies who see more mileage in battling with governments to change policies, with banks to reduce interest rates for Third World loans, and with both in some instances to cancel debts altogether, but they are few in number and this side of their work is too often overshadowed by the rest of their operation, which is giving out a different message as they try to maintain a hold on their own funding, thus transmitting conflicting signals which must make it even more difficult for those on the receiving end to know where they are.

Here too Holman's positive alternatives would rings bells for many in the Third World. He wants to see the recipients of the Telethon involved in how the money is raised, how the day is structured and in the distribution of the funds. He wants the publicity to raise the question whether the charities alleviate or reinforce racism, sexism and ageism and to challenge the way in which the TV marathons handle social problems. From recipients everywhere the cry is deafening! 'If only we could be so lucky!' [4.1]

WHY SPORT AID IS NOT ENOUGH

'Sport Aid, like Band Aid and Live Aid, provided a day of fun and a glow of achievement for millions of people. It raised money which may save the lives of some of the 18 to 20 million people who die of hunger every year. It further raised the awareness of millions of young people here about the ugly reality of hungry lives elsewhere. But what are young people supposed to do with that knowledge? Who is going to explain to them why their pity and charity change nothing?'

So wrote Victoria Brittain in 1988. She went on to say how joining in helps to reduce a little of the guilt we all feel when we see those emaciated bodies of mothers and babies on our television screens and gives us a feeling that in some small way we are trying to equal things out when in fact we know that we are not, and that when the going gets really rough television companies may well scale down their coverage, allegedly to avoid 'compassion fatigue' but more realistically to avoid admitting how little has been achieved. She concludes,

'African governments and their people are deep in the painful economic reforms the powerful Western donors asked for. But Western governments have not played their promised part in the recovery. They have not stepped up aid. Nor have they worked on a system of fair pricing for Africa's exports. Nor have they cancelled the unpayable $218 billion of Africa's debts which is draining the continent of $27 billion in interest payments every year.

If Sport Aid focused on demanding that Western governments meet their responsibilities for international economics, instead of handing them over to charities and individuals, Africa could recover its dignity and live without pity.' [4.2].

Did you know that the equivalent of all the money raised by Comic Relief has been returned to the rich countries in interest payments by the end of the annual Red Nose Day? (John Pilger) [4.3]

LEARNING THEOLOGY THE HARD WAY

On the evening of 4 September 1984 a new victim was added to the long list of dead slum-dwellers, as a result of the repressive violence. In the parish house of a low-income area, while praying and reading the psalms, Andre Jorlon was killed. For the slum-dwellers this murder was unbelievable. It seemed that the madness of death and repression, that afflicts the poor especially, knew no limits. These are the ones who suffer daily a constant violence that does not respect children, women, homes or even the church.

That is the opening paragraph from the Annual Report of the Evangelical Theological College in Santiago, Chile, 1987. They had students who lived in that slum. Two blocks away there was an army regiment. Students were often in battle with the police. Tear gas, bombings and beatings were an everyday occurrence. Telephone calls and visits from the secret police were common.

Learning theology in that environment has to be experienced to be appreciated, but it does not take much imagination to realize that the end product is likely to be very different from the one we are familiar with in the West.

The Battle for Human Rights

But then, at that time in Chile, it needed to be. Lay-people had no less a battle in the fight for human rights.

'The worst thing is when you are walking along the street . . . and all at once the police car comes by slowly and a voice says, "We know who you are and we know what you do. We are watching you!" At that moment you dash back quickly to your office, clear your desk and lie low!'

This testimony came from a Christian in the mid-1980s following the overthrow of Allende's democratically elected government. He was one of a team for whom Christian communication was more than using video in church and definitely not using modern technology to proclaim the faith and then manoeuvre people into it.

It was releasing forces in men and women living under oppression to enable them to be themselves, to take control of their life, to shape their destiny.

In any military dictatorship that can be dangerous. That was why they were being watched. They were a mix of university teachers, professors, lecturers and sociologists, nearly all of whom had been in exile after the coup of 1973, but who had returned in recent years to risk their lives in order to save others.

Video Literacy

They had made a short video to demonstrate police brutality.

Chile had two sorts of living accommodation: the *shanty town*, which by comparison with some shanty towns could look quite respectable and not a lot worse than some low-quality local authority

52

housing in Britain, and the *campamento*, where people hived off when they got too many for the shanty. They organized it, chose their patch, arrived overnight and the cardboard houses went up. Sooner or later the police moved in to destroy it.

The video showed it happening. When the police arrived the women formed a line of defence because then there could be no danger of violence. The police replied with rape.

At other times the video was an instrument of awakening. Having discovered its capacity to hold a group together they set about training people to use it, to make programmes about themselves and then to criticize and analyse their own lives.

This was video literacy, and once a group had achieved this level of self-understanding they then had to teach another group to do the same.

Songs of Protest

In a cafe on a side street in Santiago, pitch dark inside and packed tight with young people, the main entertainment was a music group. Grasping the words of songs with high amplification is not always easy, but this audience had no difficulty.

They were enjoying protest songs and poetry, well aware of what was going on in their country but still able to sing about it, even to poke fun at it but at the same time to raise serious questions.

What was the view of the authorities? 'It all depends,' they said. 'Some groups go further than others, and those who expose their views the most are most vulnerable.'

But since the messages are of necessity 'coded', like the book of Daniel contained 'coded messages' for the Jews, how many ever really got beyond the straight words and music?

'Difficult to say', they replied. 'Perhaps only 10% were politically conscious enough to discern.'

Just like many people's attitudes to the parables of Jesus, you might say.

TORTURE FIGURES

'Torture is a kind of plague which has now reached epidemic proportions. Though outlawed by the Universal Declaration of Human Rights (1948) and the Convention Against Torture (1984), to both of which all UN member states are signatories, torture is now used in over one third of the world's countries as an instrument of interrogation and systematic repression.

And though, by definition, torture is an act perpetrated by a state against an individual, it is by implication directed against whole populations — for every direct victim of torture there are many friends and relatives who wait in uncertainty and fear.

Between 1973 and 1989 there were persistent reports of torture in Chile, including the illegal detention of thousands of people without recourse to the law.

Between 1979 and 1981 Chilean human rights groups produced evidence of 311 such cases (all of which had previously been officially reported to the courts or legal notaries).

These were in addition to over 650 cases of "disappeared" people currently before the courts.

Because of the futility of such legal action (virtually no cases were actually investigated), the assumption must stand that this was merely a small representative sample of the true picture, which included killings in suspicious circumstances, random murders, internal exile and banishment without trial.

In Amnesty International's 1983 report on *Evidence of Torture in Chile*, there are studies of eighteen fully documented cases of torture between March 1980 and April 1982.' [4.4]

DEATH AND THE MAIDEN
by Ariel Dorfman

The idea for Ariel Dorfman's *Death and the Maiden* came when he was in exile from Chile in the early 1980s. The play opens with a car breakdown and the driver is offered a bed for the night by a friendly stranger. Unfortunately, the host's wife, believing she recognizes in the visitor the voice of the torturer who raped her some years before, kidnaps him and puts him on trial.

In 1990, after seventeen years of exile, Dorfman returned to Chile to settle down. Chile was then undergoing an uneasy transition to democracy. Pinochet was no longer President but he was still in charge of the armed forces. His successor appointed a commission to investigate the crimes of the dictatorship but the assumption was that the perpetrators would be neither named nor judged. The purpose was 'to heal a sick country', but they naturally found themselves having to steer a middle course between those who wanted to bury the past and those who wanted it totally exposed.

Death and the Maiden raises some interesting questions for all of us

For Insiders

1 How can the tortured and the torturer co-exist in the same land?

2 How do you heal a country traumatized by repression if the fear to speak out is still everywhere?

3 Are people free to search for justice and equality if the threat of a military intervention haunts them?

For Observers

1 Given the circumstances, can violence be avoided?

2 How guilty are we all of what happened to those who suffered most?

3 How do you handle such issues without destroying democratic stability?

Matters of Truth

1 How do you reach the truth if lying has become a habit?

2 How do you tell the truth if the mask you have adopted is identical to your face?

3 Is it legitimate to sacrifice truth to ensure peace?

4 What are the consequences of suppressing what the truth is saying to us?

General Questions

1 What difference does it make when women take power?

2 How does memory beguile, save and guide us?

3 How do we forgive those who have hurt us irreparably?

THE DISAPPEARED

One story which highlights the experience of many women living in Chile
in the early 1970s where the problems were not only
those of poverty and under-development

Alejandro Parada Gonzalez was half asleep when he heard fists pounding on his front door. It was 3 am. His wife, seven months pregnant, hauled herself our of bed to answer it.

At the door there were soldiers, asking for her husband. They forced their way in and bundled Alejandro, dressed only in his underpants, into a jeep. It was, as for so many Chileans of that time, the last anyone saw of him.

That was 1974. Nineteen years later, Alejandra's mother, Amanda, was sitting in a shabby office in central Santiago where she worked with the Association of Families of the Disappeared.

At 63, she remembered Alejandro, then a 22-year-old student of veterinary medicine, as introverted and studious, a young man with a liking for baggy sweaters and a passion for socialism.

Amanda was visiting the south of Chile when she heard of her son's disappearance. She rushed back to Santiago and spent months searching jails. Unlike some mothers, whose children were fished out of rivers or discovered in mass graves, she has never found her son's body.

In 1991, it emerged in a human rights report that Alejandro had been taken to a Santiago detention centre for political prisoners. His details are recorded in a six-line entry. 'It's the only thing we know', says his mother.

Over twenty years later the issue of Chile's more than 2,000 'disappeared' victims of Pinochet's military dictatorship will not go away despite a Chile, now enjoying spectacular economic growth and trying hard to put its past behind it.

In a speech in 1993 the President said he wanted to bring human rights to a swift conclusion and proposed the appointment of special judges to hear evidence in secret, and seek to determine the cause of death and the whereabouts of missing bodies. Nobody was to be punished. Some believe it is time to forget the past.

Amanda said the speech was a whitewash and a betrayal. Hugo O'Campo, executive secretary of the Committee for Defence of Human Rights, argued that without a proper investigation, 'society is incapable of discovering what it needs to do to make sure that these things never happen again.' [4.5]

> 'Democracy has returned now to Chile and to so many other countries where those widows resisted the military and demanded their men back.
>
> Democracy has returned, but many of those women are still waiting for the return of their fathers, their husbands, their brothers, their sons; many of them are still waiting for a river or a god to bring those bodies back from the dead.
>
> And the bodies are also waiting, somewhere; still accusing the men who murdered them, still waiting for justice to be done, still demanding to be remembered by a society that is all too willing to forget.' [4.6]

THE FIVE CENT INHERITANCE

A story of honesty, courage, faithfulness and love

Andrew Hsiao was born in 1926, the sixth of fourteen children, to a Chinese Lutheran minister, utterly dedicated to his job and to his church but nevertheless the prime cause of Andrew's rebellion against God and the church at the age of fifteen.

That was the year his father died. Andrew still remembers going into his parents' bedroom on that fateful morning. His mother lay on one bed, having just given birth to her fourteenth child and unable to get up. His father lay dead on the other.

He was the oldest child still at home. 'Andrew,' said his mother, 'your father is dead. Go through his clothes and round the house and see what money we have left! We have to bury him and we have to live on.'

It was a vain search. The Chinese economy had broken down during the Sino-Japanese War. Hitler had invaded in 1940. All mission support had ceased. Most church workers found other jobs to feed their families but Andrew's father had insisted on staying at his post — the only minister to eight churches and head of a Lutheran School with hundred of pupils — and believing the war would not last he sold everything he had inherited so that the family could survive. When things got worse his father was offered other jobs but refused to leave the flock as 'spiritual orphans'.

Finally, in one coat pocket belonging to his father he found the equivalent of 5 US cents. That was all! And Andrew cursed God for the way the family of such a faithful servant of God was now being rewarded.

Then, out of the blue and three or four years later, Andrew heard the call to the ministry. Now the problem was that he was the family breadwinner. How could he give up his job and go to college? Who would keep the family? And how could he ever tell his mother?

He still remembers clearly the day he decided he must break the news of his decision. New Year's Day 1948! He went into the kitchen where she was working. He moved around but somehow the words just wouldn't come out. 'Andrew, what's the matter?' said his mother. 'You're agitated!' The ice broken, he told her and she gave him her full support.

Months later he gave his mother all he had saved — enough rice to feed the family for six months — said his farewells, left for college in Hong Kong and they all looked forward to a reunion on his first vacation.

It was 1948. Little did he realize it would be thirty one years before he was allowed to set foot in China again. Fortunately his mother was still alive, though most of the time she was in a coma. But when his sister said, 'Mother, Andrew is back' she would come round momentarily.

Andrew has just retired as a distinguished Lutheran minister and theological teacher, and spends his time writing, teaching and preaching.

He still remembers the five cent inheritance, but it is 'no longer a sign of poverty, defeat and shame as I understood it in those days', he says; 'it has become to me a symbol of honesty, courage, faithfulness and love'.

THE TALENTED SET

Joseph

Joseph is an African, black, late thirties, with seven children. He is a graduate, married to a graduate, and the Divisional Head of a large Corporation. He drives a company car and enjoys the lifestyle of a company executive.

His home reflects his status. A guard, back and front. Rooms enormous. Furniture plush. The garden like a small park — and floodlit — and a private swimming pool worth having.

But none of it is his. It belongs to the mine. So does the car. So does the furniture. So does the privilege of sending all seven children to one of the best and most expensive schools, and the privilege of paying for them.

Joseph is a prisoner. There are other jobs he would like to do. Some he has been offered. He would like to go into academic work. But none of it is available. They could never compensate for the losses. So he is slave, with nothing to call his own.

Alice

Alice is a white Zimbabwean, who decided to use her gifts for the benefit of the black Rhodesians (as they then were) by inspiring the churches to get people reading, because Alice believed that reading was the gateway to education, health, hygiene, growth, development, social democracy, independence and self-support.

Today her organization no longer needs her, but her dream of making it self-sufficient is as much a dream as it was thirty years ago.

First they told her to get money from agencies in Europe and America so that the organization could get bigger and more successful. She did, and it was!

Then they told her that students must do projects, make money, and pay fees. So they did. They baked bread and made all sorts of things, and sold them. When that didn't do it, they told her the organization must trade and make profits, publishing and selling its own reading primers. The Americans even gave her a whole print shop to do it, but still the dream eluded her.

And towards the end of her life, when she and her colleagues discussed the problems, what they all came to see was that with their limited resources, working with the poorest in the land, in literacy and education, they could never become self-sufficient. Theirs is a world where winner takes all.

Mathilde

Mathilde grew up in the Philippines. She fought in the campaign to overthrow Marcos and install Cory Aquino. She is not poor and she is not dim. She is highly educated, with considerable resources, but she felt poor because she had no power.

And what she was saying throughout that campaign was, 'We may not have much (power) but we will hang on to what little we have. We will not have this man to rule over us, and we will not play his game.

Why? Because he is hard and cruel. He reaps where other people have done all the sowing. He gathers when other people have done all the work. He is a thief in courtly garb. His wife's wardrobe is bulging with shoes, and our hard-earned cash is being salted away in his Swiss bank account.'

Mathilde may not have much but she will at least keep it until the system changes.

WHY CAN'T THE INDIANS BE LIKE EVERYBODY ELSE?

'I don't know why it is, but we seem to be able to work like this anywhere else in the world but never in India. Why? I guess it must be something to do with the Indian ego.'

'I'm not sure it's the Indian ego. It may have something to do with the American way of doing things.'

'Maybe, and I guess we both have to take responsibility for that.'

The first speaker was American, the second Indian. They obviously knew each other well because they could speak so freely and they never got anywhere near blows. I was sitting in front of them on a public bus and couldn't help overhearing the conversation.

The American wanted a big evangelical campaign in Bombay. To achieve it he needed Indian co-operation, but not much.

The Indian wanted to consider the issues, to find out what else was going on in Bombay and what plans for evangelism the churches already had. The American wasn't interested. It didn't matter what the others were doing. There was still room for another effort and he intended to make it.

The Indian wanted to get together a group of people out of which the American might construct his campaign. The American wanted to go in with a big splash and then create a small group to continue the work.

The Indian wanted to go cautiously and slowly and carry people with him. The American wanted a big explosion and hoped that things would be different afterwards.

The Indian wanted a controlled experiment. The American wanted to get on with the action.

And so the argument continued until the American exploded and accused the Indian of having too big an ego. It was just as well he was wrong or the Indian might have exploded too.

But the American was hardly right when he said that for that they must share the responsibility equally. The Indian was surely right to want to do things his own way in his country. I wondered if the Americans would have worn it in Washington!

'You can only help one of your luckless brothers by trampling down a dozen others' (Brecht)

THE CUTTING EDGE

The Indian Society for Promoting Christian Knowledge (ISPCK), Delhi, was started in the early eighteenth century by SPCK and did not become fully independent until 1970.

ISPCK is a publishing house, committed first to the Anglican Church and then to the Church of North India but now enjoying partnerships with a wide variety of groups including CSI, Baptists, theological colleges, Bible Society, the National Council of Churches in India and the World Council of Churches in Geneva.

For many years much of their material was subsidized, not always widely used, and bishops and parishes were often less active than they might have been in promoting it. Nor were they helped by the fact that they had to publish in English, Hindi, Urdu, Punjabi, Marathi and Gujurati, but today they have achieved a large measure of self-sufficiency and can boast 60% of the market share in the Protestant arena.

Originally concerned primarily with liturgical material, their current publishing programme has developed at two levels to reflect their Christian concern for the whole of life:

1 Issues of general development in India (rural poverty, bonded labour, better health).

2 A regional language programme of popular literature at low prices of interest to people in villages covering such topics as Aids, drugs, alcohol, the family, the place of women, caste and dowry, education, agriculture and poetry.

THE CHANGING FACE

The Latin American Biblical Seminary, San José, Costa Rica, was founded in 1923, received government recognition as a university (with Schools of Biblical and Theological Sciences) in 1997, and began building a new campus financed by women and men around the world, rich and poor, honouring the names of women, one dollar per name.

The university serves a network of centres and churches throughout Latin America and the Caribbean with over 2,000 students who combine residential, extension and independent studies at the B.Th, Licenciatura, and M.Th levels. The central library of 28,000 volumes and 150 periodicals will soon be accessible, along with other major theological libraries in the region, through the Internet.

Centro Evangelico Latinoamericano de Estudios Pastorales (CELEP), also began in San José, and serves Brazil, Peru, Ecuador, Central America and Mexico. Its commitments are similar but different, not competitive but complementary.

It is breaking new theological ground, particularly in non-formal theological education, sees itself as an enabling organization and has a series of publications, studies and programmes reflecting its concerns.

Conscientization is a keyword, covering social projects, radio programmes for women and the needs of indigenous peoples. Always committed to work with the people at the bottom, they were shaken recently to discover another level well below the one at which they are working!

Civil Disobedience

How do you respond to a repressive or corrupt government? If it is a dictatorship, dissension may lead to torture or imprisonment or both. If it is a democracy, you will be expected to stay within the bounds of civil disobedience.

Read Daniel 3 and 6 (resistance), Romans 13: 1-7 (submission) and I Maccabees 2: 29-48 (tension).

Focus on one or two recent examples of civil disobedience in your immediate environment. Weigh the issues. Reflect on the methods used and the consequences. Notice how often nothing happens until civil disobedience crosses the line, and also how in a time of strong and unreasonable government civil disobedience becomes acceptable to a wider section of society.

Daniel and Maccabees demonstrate two points where the shoe pinches and help to sharpen the two kinds of people who engage in it.

In fifth century Babylon (Daniel) there were Jews in exile who had adjusted and done well out of the system. Perhaps Daniel was one of them, in a high position at court. Some of them were doing too well in the eyes of those Babylonians who found life tough. It is the tension between the immigrant community and the natives! Hence their attempt to turn the screw. Nothing too serious. Just an edict or two to test their loyalty. A few stupid regulations, but enough to cause discomfort.

In second century Greece (Maccabees) the problem is the change from a religious-based society (Judaism) to a secular one (Greece). Jewish life, morals, holidays, etc. all arose from their religion. The king was Yahweh's representative. And most Jews knew it and accepted it even if they did not always recognize it. The new controls were secular state controls and the Jews didn't like it.

In both cases the question was: how far do you go before you rebel, and when you rebel how far do you carry your rebellion? Recent history teaches us something of the cost. The story of Bonhoeffer during the Second World War is a good example. The ground is fairly well trodden. What Dorfman explores in *Death and the Maiden* is what happens when the attempts to crush any resistance go too far.

But he also raises a number of other questions. Recent events in Chile, alongside Daniel and the Maccabees, and Dorfman's play (and if you cannot see it, read it) help us to appreciate what is happening in many places, but then (thanks again to the mirror!) they also help us to see ourselves.

Death and the Maiden gives us three characters: one who is guilty of cruelty and torture and tries to pretend it never happened (Roberto), one who seeks vengeance (Paulina) and one who is anxious to do nothing that may mar his chances of a new life and so tries to avoid involvement on the grounds that we have to forget the past and build bridges (Gerardo). Which one is me?

'A fragile democracy is strengthened by expressing, for all to see, the deep dramas and sorrows and hopes that underlie its existence and it is not by hiding the damage we have inflicted on ourselves that we will avoid its repetition' (Ariel Dorfman).

'For every individual we see there are whole societies in pain. The people we see are the very tips of vast icebergs and they are carrying all of that with them. They need us to bear witness to what has been done. If we refuse to take notice we are joining the torturer. Here we see the walking wounded: the real casualties are those we don't see' (Caroline Gorst-Unsworth). [4.7]

Parable of the Talents

Read the parable in Matthew (25: 14-30) and compare it with Luke (19: 11-27) where the emphasis is more on power than on money. Work out what difference this makes.

Imagine life in a theological college like the one in Santiago. Enter into the feelings of Andre Jorlon and the slum-dwellers. Sense the dangers of those who work for human rights in that sort of situation.

Put that side by side with a situation in which CEDECO (the South American equivalent of the Sunday School Union or National Council for Christian Education) was producing comics for children telling the story of Moses and the slaves in Egypt. When children took them home and their parents read them they realized that they were not reading about Egypt 4000 years ago, but about themselves, today.

The local bishop said it was a misinterpretation of the Bible, which was being read against the background of their own culture, and part of a communist plot to start a revolution. His critics replied that that is what he would have said if he had been around in the time of Moses, because if you are a slave and you read a story about the deliverance of the slaves you can hardly be blamed if you think it might apply to you.

But can you in fact read the Bible at all except against your own culture? The problem is not that we read it against our own culture but that we are not always aware how many of our interpretations are tied to our culture so that we find it difficult to appreciate interpretations which arise in different circumstances.

Make a list of the underlying Western twentieth century assumptions that lie behind this parable. For example,

— that because a man has resources he can give orders and others must obey

— that working hard, or making money, or being successful are what life is all about

— that increasing the GNP, doubling your money, making your pile, living on borrowed reserves or mortgages which eventually have to be paid because they were never yours anyway, is a satisfactory way of living.

Take a fresh look at the way in which the parable is usually interpreted and consider how much we interpret it against our culture and use it to reinforce the things we believe.

List the questions we never ask. For example,

— why five for one, two for another and one for another?

— why is it better to gamble with something that is not your own rather than hold it in trust and take care of it?

— how to double your money without someone else losing it?

— when you have done exactly what you were told and been commended why does all the reward go to someone else?

— when you have done nothing wrong with what you were given, why lose it to someone else?

Identify the character. Who is the master in the story? A dictator in a military regime? A landlord? A managing director or a bishop? Or is he the personification of the people who hold power and resources, or even 'the system'.

Use the experience of 'the talented set' to enter into the experience of others and imagine what they feel and think when they read this parable.

Joseph was clearly given five talents and he went out and got five more. Alice may not have had five but she did have two, and thanks to her efforts they became four, if not forty-four. Mathilde is at the bottom. She has one talent. What are we to make of her response?

Things to Do

CORRIDOR OF POVERTY

Take a map of the world. Draw a line at 10° and another at 40° longitude, both north of the equator. Take a close look at the countries which fall in-between. You are now looking at the world's poorest people. Four out of five of the world's poor live there. What does this corridor of poverty say to those who live outside it?

Share your concerns with a small group for a limited period — once a month or six weeks straight off. Ask each member to choose one region, country or city and find out all they can about it — population, language, food, trade, religion, economy. Then share your discoveries and discuss what you feel about them.

In the last session but one ask yourselves:

1 What has it done to me as a person to have focused on one corner of the world to try to understand it better?

2 To what extent have my attitudes to that region, or to the issues which have come out of it, changed as a result?

3 How many times have I found myself reading press articles, hearing news items on the radio or watching programmes on TV which, without that concentration of thought and feeling, I may never have noticed?

In the final session consider what is the most meaningful thing you can actually *do*, either as group or as individuals. Make it as specific and personal as you can, even if it is small or simple.

Avoid the obvious 'we must pray for them' or 'we should write a cheque for a charity', so that somebody else does something. Stay with it even if it is painful. Indeed, that could be your true prayer and more effective than a quick word or a quick fix. That is what suffering prayer is about. [4.8]

MONOPOLY

Everyone who has played Monopoly knows that the result depends almost entirely on what you are dealt at the beginning and what you have the good luck to acquire in the first half-hour. After that, there is little you can do. If all you have is Old Kent Road and the Waterworks, don't expect to win. If you have Pall Mall and Mayfair, a green and a couple of reds, you are in with a chance.

The idea is not original but try working out your own ways to intensify the point.

eg   re-designate the properties (Old Kent Road to Bangladesh, Mayfair to USA, etc), based on the corridor of poverty, with three sides of the board for the poor and one side for the rich.

allocate a third to a half of the properties before the game begins, drawing lots but ensuring that each player only has properties from one side of the board. Allow players to purchase the rest in the usual way.

allocate money from the bank so that those with the poorest properties (lowest costs) receive 10%, those on the second side 20%, those on the third side 30%, and the richest 40%.

Encourage those with wealth to be kind and considerate, occasionally to waive rents or make a gift, often to make loans, always to charge interest. Instead of people going out of the game allow them simply to run up debts to the wealthier players.

Once you get the idea work out your own variations and add all sorts of other twists. It could be a very short game, but it is important to stick with it for the time it normally takes if only to feel the tedium of enduring or trying to solve interminable problems.

Ask some questions. How did players feel, both at the beginning when they knew the rules and again at the end? How did the rich try to help and with what results? What would have to be done to give the losers a chance?

PRISONER OF THE LORD

The courage and sufferings of others, especially in Third World situations or in other circumstances of acute distress, raise a number of questions which may be the subject of personal prayer and spiritual growth, of group discussion or of public worship.

1 What spiritual resources are needed to survive and how can we cultivate them?

One way is to make your own list: what hymns, Bible readings, books, biographies, music, memories would you need? What would you think about? Who would you pray for? What would you hope for?

2 Meditate on the price some people pay for their mere existence, never mind their faith, and consider how much attention we give to their spiritual, moral and physical resources. What have they to teach us and how can they encourage us? How dare we 'esteem them not, smitten of God and afflicted' (Isa. 53: 3-4)? Third World people, poor, ignorant and in need of our charity. Afflicted!

3 Consider how their stories present a different dimension of the Third World which TV, the media, the churches, charities and aid agencies so rarely tell us anything about.

Try to work out the differences between the two sorts of stories and find reasons why these stories are not told and others are. Has it something to do with drama, disaster, large-scale events, the media or fund-raising?

Ask yourself which has the greatest influence on you, and how far your concerns are genuine and deep and how much you are just being motivated by the latest media campaign. There is nothing wrong with that, but it is important to understand the difference.

4 Should we talk less of 'development' as if it were a panacea for troubles and talk more of human resources?

Food for Thought — Food for Prayer

FAITH AND CULTURE

Pray for Christian groups in Chile, in their concern to establish and maintain links between faith and culture

— for local churches, essentially poor and open to all the people in the community, who want to see themselves as maintaining strong links between faith and culture

— for larger institutional churches, who would like to support their local churches in their response to the needs of the poor but whose hierarchy have too much to lose by way of investments and resources

— for food programmes, whereby people express what they believe about nutrition as they share their money with one another to buy food wholesale and so get it cheaper

— for child recreation programmes, whereby young people express what they believe about community and education as they give their time to play with children and help with developments such as literacy, music, scientific research and handicrafts

— for women's projects, which identify biblical themes on women and help them to develop handicrafts so as to increase their income.

Consider ways in which we in our society might pay more attention to the links between our faith, culture and communication.

Pray for those professionally involved in both spheres and especially for those who are trying to relate the one to the other.

FAITH AND COMMUNICATION

Pray for other Christian groups in Chile, in their concern to establish and maintain links between faith and communication.

— for those organizations committed to building bridges between communication and culture

— for community development programmes, where the purpose is to animate people to an understanding of what is happening around them and to take action about it

— for publishing programmes, including teaching manuals for the poor and the fruits of academic research to persuade government bodies to adopt policies in favour of the poor

— for radio programmes, where broadcasters are working hard to transform commercial radio into community radio, and (where they cannot) to improve the community output

— for television awareness programmes, to sharpen people's critical faculty as to what they are being offered, especially where the only source of television is government television

— for self-made video programmes, for social and educational purposes and to stimulate people to 'see' themselves and to ask questions about their quality of life

— for popular theatre programmes to produce literature on the community as a living body.

Category
Theological Books, Study Guides, Social and Moral Affairs

Remember
Reviewers and editors of journals and periodicals
politicians, the media and people of other faiths

Focus On
an occasion when your view was challenged and changed by something you read
and give thanks for writers with a different approach which made it possible

---

TALENT SPOTTING

Identify people with one talent in today's world who are saying, 'We don't just want quick profits, or a few improvements, and certainly not a hand-out — but how do we get a different social system?' Why do you think some people take 'a different view?'

Identify people with two talents who struggle to make things work, often against tremendous odds.

Identify 'the winners' too! To what extent are they also victims? White as well as black in South Africa? Rich as well as poor? Employed as well as unemployed?

Pray for each group in turn and (possibly after a short discussion) seek guidance as to how any of us may achieve change.

Pray For Translators

who seek not so much to use different words
as to take the words, grammar, history, culture, environment and experience of one world
and convey it all in the words of another

EASTER
A Time to Explore

Theme

When I am weak, then I am strong.

II Cor 12: 10 (REB)

To contemplate the sufferings of others ('what befalls them') is to feel their sense of weakness — their utter powerlessness. Whatever Jesus said or did, he was no match for the power of Judaism or the Roman Empire.

From one point of view he had no need to suffer or die. In many similar situations he might well have got away with what he said and did for ages. Indeed, had they left him alone, he might well have continued into a ripe old age and we might never have heard of him! But that is beside the point!

What matters is that the decision was not his. Power decides. Weakness accepts. And when preachers tell us that he was in control and that 'he reigned from the tree' they are not so much making a statement about his ability to control as about God's capacity to take hold of what is done to him and use it for a nobler purpose. Through him the powerless find hope, not so much in what they can do but in what God can do through them.

It is not difficult to see why 'resurrection' was the word chosen to describe the indescribable, but try to feel what it means to those who experience his feelings of powerlessness to the point where they begin to feel that the miracle is happening to them.

This is to begin to understand the strength that comes in weakness (I Cor 1: 18-31). Sadly, the church in the West, and most of Western society with it, has always found it difficult to remember. Ever since Constantine, the growth of the church and the natural instinct to create large institutions, the church (with rare exceptions like St Francis) has always been in danger of opting for the power that goes with strength rather than discovering the strength that flows from weakness.

Many people in the developing nations know better. To share their experience of 'awaking' (being made to stand up) will enable us not only to get a different picture of them but also to rediscover our own roots through them.

key word	*anastasis* is normally translated 'resurrection' but if you do that you find yourself all too easily trotting down the old road, recognizing the old signs, stumbling over the same old obstacles and with no eyes to see something new it might have to say. Literally, in classical Greek particularly, it means 'making to stand up', 'making to rise and leave their place', and from that it comes to mean 'awakening' or even 'rising up'.
αναστασις Make to stand	

Who are the Poor?

Let us assume that when we refer to 'the poor' in today's world we all know what we mean and we all mean the same people — aid agencies and the media use the term to refer to the Third World in general, the mass of needy people within the poorer or less-developed nations, the urban poor or less-well-off in Western society, refugees and victims of natural disasters who have lost all their possessions. And when the tin for the poor is rattled under our noses it would never occur to us to ask who the poor were and in many cases would be thought offensive if we did. But the position may not be nearly so clear-cut and we may once again miss the reality by making the wrong assumptions. Who, for example, are the poor in the Bible?

By the time we get to the later books of the Old Testament, such as Proverbs, 'the poor' tends to refer to the feckless; the people who are poor as a result of laziness. But this is a secondary usage. Primarily, 'the poor' refers to those people who are the victims of social injustice. That is why they are poor. Even Proverbs 13: 23 does not lose sight of this. True, they are needy and unable to provide themselves with the essentials of life, but the underlying problem is that they are without power and at the same time abused by those who hold it.

The causes are not very different from those of today. In older biblical communities, with a simple life-style, poverty was less of a problem. Everything belonged to the clan. With the arrival of the monarchy and the city, a settled rather than a nomadic existence and the sight of luxury goods, greed, corruption and oppression soon crept in. Over-taxation and forced labour made some people poor. Wars, raids and invasions made others poor. In other cases it was the economy and especially economic conflict. Bad seasons, crop failure and loss of cattle. Land-grabbing and money-lending with excessively high rates of interest. Deprive people of a viable relationship with the land and you not only cut off their wages but you also make them vulnerable. They become wage-earners who cannot earn wages or employees who are unemployed, until in the end they are unemployable. And when the going is tough certain groups in all societies seem to find themselves most threatened: widows, orphans, sojourners and resident aliens with no landed rights.

The Old Testament has four words for 'poor', and if we want to see ourselves as 'sensitive to the poor' they tell us much about the sort of people we need to be on the look out for.

dal refers to people low in status, the lower class lacking the wealth and prestige of the upper class.

ani refers to the pain of oppression, people who are powerless and unable to resist the socially powerful, with a special emphasis on the pain or oppression caused by material poverty. (The root of the word *ani* means 'to oppress or afflict').

ebyon means a person in dire want, lacking basic food and clothing and entirely dependent on others.

rus means deep poverty, especially in the lower classes.

What they all have in common is people of low social status, lacking basic resources, rights, respect and a place in society, and therefore vulnerable to those in power and defenceless against those above them.

In the New Testament we have *penes*, meaning poor in relation to the well-to-do (i.e. unable to make a living from property and therefore dependent on a wage) and *ptochos* meaning 'reduced to a beggarly situation' or just plain 'dependent'.

But again, the prevalent groups are widows, orphans, sojourners and resident aliens with no landed rights. The emphasis almost always falls on material poverty and when we are tempted to spiritualize poverty, as for instance in interpreting the Beatitudes, perhaps we should ask ourselves why.

These are the poor to whom biblical society acknowledges a responsibility. Yahweh hears their cry and will save them (Psalm 12: 5). He always has. The whole thrust of the Exodus demonstrated his commitment to the slaves, the non-persons of Egyptian society at that point in history. They are the ones who are to be made strong (Lev 25: 35). The Law must be structured so as to pay attention to social matters that affect the poor (Ex 23: 11). Interest on loans must be restricted (Lev 23: 36) and debts must be cancelled at appropriate time intervals (Deut 23: 24-5). The New Testament goes further with its emphasis on 'open-handed sharing'. The gospel is ' good news for the poor' (Luke 4: 18; 7: 22).

But if the Bible helps us to 'find' the poor, can the poor help us to re-discover the Word? Ceresko points out how readers in Latin America were quick to spot the connection between their own social conditions and the social conditions of the people they were reading about. Newly-formed base communities in particular found a variety of meanings, but the significance and relevance of the exodus was not lost on them, and from that emerged 'the hermeneutical principle of the poor'. Reading the Bible through the eyes of the poor and the powerless — trying to understand it and interpret it as it seems to those who are 'at the bottom' socially and economically — is an experience which can not only open our eyes and hearts to the poor but also give us new insight into the biblical message.

To achieve this, Ceresko argues, we need to understand better how the Bible treats history. The Books of Samuel and Kings treat history much as we do (i.e. about kings, rulers and important people in society) but Genesis 12-50 is the history of their births, marriages and deaths, migrations, hopes, fears and conflicts. This is how early history saw itself. This is where the action lies. This is where the really important things are happening — among people outside the major centres of influence and decision making — the people on the margin!

When we read the Bible through their eyes we begin to see what Yahweh is doing through them and what he is saying to us through them. And the gospel of resurrection (or standing up) is not about changing the poor into the rich, or the weak into the powerful, or indeed helping them to become the kind of people that we think God wants them to be. It is much more about exploring their life so that once we see what it is that God is doing *there* we may have a better understanding of what he is doing elsewhere and how best we can fit in with him. [5.1]

EXPLODING MYTHS

Even in the Third World there are no 'hungry countries'. There are only poor people living in them who cannot grow enough, or buy enough, food to meet their needs. In this respect there is no difference between a developed and an under-developed country.

****

World hunger is not caused by population pressures although these do aggravate the situation . . . Nor is hunger a result of the 'climate' or the 'weather' . . . even if climate can also be an exacerbating factor.

****

Flood or drought can help to create the conditions under which famine thrives — but they do not create the human action and inaction that insures that the wealthy alone will eat — come hell or high water. [5.2]

STRENGTH AND WEAKNESS IN A BANANA REPUBLIC

If you suffer from a feeling of weakness and powerlessness and are looking for hope, Costa Rica is probably one of the more likely places to look in South and Central America. Travel brochures certainly make it sound attractive. It may not seem quite like that if you live there.

Imagine you are a literacy teacher in San José. Today is International Literacy Day and you are off to a celebration over 100 miles away at Rio Frior. Fifty students at least are to receive their awards and are full of hope in a difficult situation.

You leave the quiet city of San José, 3000 feet above sea level, in the darkness around five o'clock in the morning. You climb twice as high, over the mountains before descending to the heat of the tropical rain forest at sea level. At best you are travelling at about 25 mph, so prepare for a five-hour journey each way.

As the sun comes up, and you drive through the villages, you get your first display of power. This may be a democratic country facing an election, but there are only two parties, both Conservative, and 71% of the land is owned by thirty seven families. Every family displays their little flag — not *their* little flag but the little flag of the party supported by the land-owner. Workers here are neither rebellious nor Marxist — they are very passive. It would never do to suggest anything but loyalty — not if they wanted to keep their house, that is!

After driving through fields of sugar beet and coffee plantations, all belonging to one family, you reach the lower levels where all you see is bananas! Everywhere! Huge bunches, all tied up in plastic bags while still on the trees, partly for protection from insects and partly as a dating procedure.

Then comes the second display of power, because if the bananas are controlled, organized and protected, so too are the workers, only in their case 'the plastic bag' is a house provided by the banana company. Indeed, you may feel there is nothing here at all but what the banana companies provide. In fairness, the houses look reasonable habitations, but one can never be yours, and all stand in stark contrast with the swimming pool mansion luxury of the directors' homes on the same plantation.

Alongside power is weakness. The last twenty miles or so is rough and calls for a four-wheeled drive. Public transport is non-existent. You pick up three people, going to the same event. They had been walking for ninety minutes and always under threat of a tropical thunderstorm. One had an hour's walk each way for every class he attended.

Literacy, for these people, is a great deal more than learning to read. It is a key to development, a passport to a different way of life. As they learn to read they learn also about health and hygiene, nutrition and cooking. In some cases their reading programme is carefully designed to stimulate them to see what is wrong in their situation, to analyse causes and to commit themselves to change.

For years missionaries and aid workers have been saying it. Education and literacy are basic human rights, tools to enable people to assume responsibility for their own life, to shape their destiny and that of their family. So before long it must surely have something to do with the state of the roads, the houses, the conditions of employment, and the politics of those thirty seven families who own 71% of the land.

Weakness may yet prove stronger than strength!

RADIO AS AN AGENT OF CHANGE

Radio, not less than literature, may be used for the benefit of popular education and as a means of achieving human dignity, self-determination and human rights.

That is why churches working among Quechua peasants in Peru have taken to it.

The Quechua live in remote rural areas and are very dependent on the land for their livelihood. The Peruvian government regularly passes legislation that affects them, but because of their remoteness, because they can neither read nor speak Spanish (in which the legislation is written), and because they probably couldn't understand the technical legal language if they did, they have little or no awareness of what is to happen to them until it happens.

Hence the need to take the legislation, simplify it, translate it and broadcast it, which is exactly what the churches tackled. They then used radio to start a discussion. Most villages have one person who can write, and in five years they received 15,000 letters and 250 cassettes from the Quechua giving opinions and ideas on government developments affecting their life.

The programme also provided a basis for a wider education. When the government had a programme on forestation or health, for example, the churches were able to take it, simplify it and relate to the Quechua where they are. To information they could then add motivation, because it is no use telling people how to plant trees if they don't see the point of it in the first place.

As the work developed they needed to link up various radio groups. They selected five, one on the north coast, two between the desert and the jungle, one in Sierra and one in the jungle, in the hope that they could use material prepared for one station in some of the others.

In a country with such difficult communications, however, one of the problems was actually finding the technical means whereby one station could communicate with another. But this didn't stop each station getting along on its own, and in a regular morning programme lasting an hour it is quite common for these peasants to be chatting away about their problems, their alternatives, what the government is planning and how the new legislation will affect them.

The five areas represent quite a variety of different people with different problems, concerns and solutions, so each area has its own news and each addresses its own issues. In one situation, for example, peasants who had become small landowners found themselves in difficulties when it came to bargaining with others, and the old landlords were standing by all ready to buy up the land again. These peasants needed to exchange views, to help one another and to establish a solidarity if they are to cope with their problem.

General education also features in the programme. Primary schooling leaves a lot to be desired. What is needed is *rural* education. Most education comes from Lima and is based on Western standards as well as being in Spanish. It shows little respect for local culture or agriculture on which these people depend. So the churches have been getting the peasants in twenty areas to write about the links between rural education and culture and then broadcasting the issues over the radio.

MUSIC AS AN AGENT OF CHANGE

Asian words, Asian music
for the Asian people
— and for the fullness
of Asian worship

Dr Francisco Feliciano has a reputation as the conductor of the Manila Philharmonic Orchestra and has conducted orchestras in Japan, Germany and the USA. He is also a composer and hymn writer. One of his contributions, the eucharistic hymn 'Far beyond our mind's grasp', is included in the most recent Baptist hymnbook, *Baptist Praise and Worship* (OUP, 1991).

But when he is at home in Manila, in the Philippines, he is the Director of the Asian Institute for Liturgy and Music. The Institute is his brainchild. He started it in 1980 to develop Asian music within the Asian churches and to counter Western imports, some of which he regards as second-best in an Asian context. The Christian Conference of Asia gave him their backing.

Due partly to history and colonialization, many Asian churches are still largely dependent on traditional Western hymns and music, including Western musical instruments like the organ.

Due partly to the power of Western music in general through today's media, coupled with the strength of Western Christian music at international conferences, charismatic choruses and music from the West are sweeping through the Asian churches.

If Asia had no Christian music of her own this would hardly be a helpful and creative process. But many Asian Christian leaders see Christianity in Asia going back at least as far as that of the West and some of Asia's musical skills, instruments and expressions are older. They are also different and naturally more suited to Asian needs and life.

Five members of staff from the Institute, therefore, travel widely in Asia, collecting material which they then record and publish at a cost of around £2,000 a time. At the last count their list of forthcoming publications included choral anthems and Hakka songs from Taiwan, some new hymns from Korea, and both hymns and liturgical material from the North Philippines. They also hoped to publish 250 new Asian hymns for the Christian Conference of Asia. Only the shortage of money, not the shortage of Asian material, restricts their output.

The Institute also has a large collection of Asian musical instruments, which they encourage churches to use as a variation on the organ, and over sixty full time students from Malaysia, Thailand, Singapore, Taiwan, Indonesia and Burma. Half their students are composers, many are involved in choral work, some are interested in musicology, some are organists, some training to be singers and teachers of music.

AN ASIAN HYMN

Far beyond our mind's grasp
    and our tongue's declaring,
you are here in mystery,
    quietly, truly, without fail;
lifted once on Calvary,
    sin and weakness bearing,
O Lord, how wondrously
    you call us through the veil.

None of us is worthy
    of your gracious presence
in this meal together,
    yet the gift is yours by choice.
In the face of death,
    in you is safe dependence,
your promise is for life;
    we only can rejoice.

So our hearts are lifted
    to the realms above us,
nourished and united
    by the precious bread and wine:
here what sweet contentment,
    knowing that you love us!
We thank you for this feast,
    this fellowship divine.

Soon you bid us scatter,
    share what we inherit
from this home of blessing
    where we taste your peace and
                        grace:
may our lives be altars
    glowing with your Spirit
to light the lamps of those
    who also seek your face.

Francisco Feliciano, paraphrased by James Minchin (b.
1942). Tr. The Christian Conference of Asia (*Baptist Praise
and Worship*, 432). The tune is Caturog Na Nonoy, a
Bicolano folk melody from the Philippines, arr. by
Lawrence Bartlett (b. 1933).

THE CHEEK OF IT!

It was 5 o'clock in the morning. An Englishman and an American couple were standing side-by-side in a queue at Delhi to check in for a flight that left at 8. Not surprisingly, they were surrounded by people in Asian dress. But then all at once a group of Buddhist monks with shaven head and saffron robes appeared. It was too much for the American woman, who turned to the Englishman and said, 'You really do get some weird characters here, don't you?'

The Englishman looked nonplussed, if not embarrassed, so, nothing daunted and before he could respond, she went on, 'It's all right as long as they stay in their own country and don't come to ours.'

What he really felt was not clear. What was clear was that he couldn't take that when he knew that both of them were visitors to Asia, both looked rather odd in their Western dress, and when he reflected on what Europeans and Americans had inflicted on Asia over a couple of centuries, so he went into battle.

'Oh, I don't know,' he was heard to say, 'it might enrich us!'

It was a conversation stopper. She turned in the other direction without saying a word. A slow check-in took the best part of three hours and the plane took off late. But neither spoke to the other again.

NEW LEADERSHIP FOR SOUTH AFRICA

Thabo Mbeki on Racism and Poverty

Thabo Mbeki, President of theANC and Executive Deputy President of South Africa, paid a return visit to Sussex University in the autumn of 1995 to receive an Honorary Doctor of Laws. His first visit was as an undergraduate in 1962, the first black South African to study there.

The university's links with South Africa were strengthened in the early 1970s when the Students' Union and the University founded the Mandela Scholarship to enable students from South Africa and Namibia who had been denied access to higher education in their own countries to study at Sussex.

One result is that Sussex now has more alumni in the South African parliament (four) than in Westminster and several more who are senior civil servants in the Mandela administration. Educating young South Africans has indeed been one important aspect of the University's involvement in the creation of the New South Africa.

On the eve of the first multiracial elections in South Africa, a Watchnight Service and Prayer Vigil was held in the University Meeting House from 10.30 to midnight. Picking up an idea from a Methodist Church in Johannesburg which had kept a candle surrounded by barbed wire burning against the day of liberation, a candle surrounded by barbed wire formed the major symbol at that service and at midnight the barbed wire was ceremonially removed, reminding some present of the crown of thorns and the suffering that preceded the resurrection.

Next day, the South African Students' Society, the Black Students' Society and the Students' Union and staff of the University held a simple ceremony to mark the occasion byplanting a commemorative tree, symbol of new life, at a focal point on the campus.

It all looked very different from that day in 1964 when the University virtually closed and the citizens of Brighton observed a moment of silence as students marched from Brighton to London to fight for the lives of Nelson Mandela and others who stood in danger of being sentenced to death by the courts of the white tyranny in South Africa.

It all looked very different then for Thabo Mbeki. He had come to Sussex only because a South African woman had insisted that if the leadership of the ANC knew what was good for him, they needed to ensure that he was better educated. His reluctance was met with a concession that his future could be negotiated at the end of his first year. He stayed for four years because that same leadership insisted that at least he must have a Master's degree.

But when he became a full-time activist against apartheid and addressed rallies all over the world, 'not once,' he said in his acceptance speech, 'did anybody during that multitude of meetings ask me about what the University had so diligently taught us, the laws of supply and demand.' No wonder he had doubts!

The removal of the crown of thorns and the new life of the 'resurrection' in this case took not three days but thirty years, but then as Thabo Mbeki 'stood tall', he continued,

'If it was possible thus to succeed against what was considered the modern fountain-head of racism in the world, it should be impermissible to look for excuses why this scourge cannot be defeated wherever it raises its venomous head.

And yet our common task is not yet accomplished, for there remains still the responsibility to wipe out the legacy of racism which continues to cling to all parts of our body politic and to confront the racism that we find in many parts of the developed world, which will not go away if it is not combated in a conscious and purposeful manner.

Its twin brother is poverty, the existence of that condition which leads to such corruption of the soul that it becomes easy to take another person's life, to seize their goods and to comfort oneself by saying that they, being of a different colour or race or ethnicity, were not, in any case, as human as me.

The creation of a better life for all, the achievement of freedom from poverty, thus become part of the common historic mission which said to all of us at this University, as we confronted the challenge of the apartheid system, that we would do a great disservice to everything good that the human intellect has produced, if all we did was merely to stand and wait.

We do not believe we would be wrong if we said that among the great problems of the new century that will soon be upon us will be those of poverty and racism. I believe that, together, we have demonstrated that we have the will to overcome.'

WHAT IT IS TO LOVE

To love someone is not first of all to do things for people, because we can do things for people and reveal to them that they're incapable; we can do things for people and crush them! We can do things for people and just make them feel they're no good.

To love someone essentially is to reveal to them their beauty; to love someone is not so much to give them of our riches, as to give to the other their riches. It is to help people to stand up, to help people trust themselves. That's why we always say about people in developing countries 'do not give fish, give a fishing rod!' It is **to help people to stand up** — to have pride in themselves, to discover their dignity, their value, the gift that is theirs; to discover their beauty, the meaning of their lives, their purpose in the world.

So, to love someone is very simple; you don't have to have a lot of things. It's a way of looking, it's a way of listening, it's a way of appreciating. When we know that we are loved we feel safe.

How will we know that we are loved ? It's the tone of voice, it's the way we respond to each other's needs. The tone of voice reveals anger or it reveals love. The tone of voice can say, 'You really annoy me. I wish you weren't around.' That's the third time you've woken we up during the night!' The tone of voice says a lot — just as the body says a lot!

When we hold someone, the vibrations that come from our bodies are totally different if we are at peace with them, from if we are angry or upset. What happens if we sense at one moment 'I am not loved'? We can all pick this up; equally, we can sense, 'I am loved'.

To love someone is very simple and it is very profound. Love is the greatest gift of God. [5.3]

IN *STEP* WITH BEDAN

A Vision for a Christian Magazine in Africa

The creation of *Step* in Kenya in the early 1980s was an important landmark in the development of African Christian literature. It was to become *the* magazine for young African Christians throughout the continent. The very vision was unrealistic once you thought about Africa's postal services, languages and currency problems. But that deterred neither the tiny group of enthusiastic African Christians, whose brainchild it was, nor Youth for Christ, who nurtured it.

One of the visionaries, Bedan Mbugwa, was a young fellow in his early thirties who as a child had spent many nights lying in the bushes near to his family home in Kenya. That was where his parents took him and his two brothers when the fighting got too close. He can still remember the sound of gunfire between the British colonialists and the rebel freedom fighters. When he was six he hid there for the last time. That night every hut in the village was burned. Weeks later he learned that both his parents had been killed.

What was not killed was the faith his mother had taught him and the knowledge of scripture handed out at the local Baptist church. That faith and his experience in the bush gave him vision and inspiration. As he grew up two things grabbed him.

One was the potential and resourcefulness of the people of his own generation, but he knew too that they needed leadership to become productive.

In one village he noticed people walking three miles to the river for water. But none of them was so poor that they couldn't afford to pay one Kenya shilling for it. So he shared his concern with his friends. Together they found a couple of large wheels and a disused drum. With a little ingenuity and a lot of hard work they made a water carrier, and one man was soon earning 4,000 Kenya shillings a year fetching water. 'A good salary,' he said, 'even in the city!'

He then saw that the key was education and communication, so he took himself off to the States to study journalism. When he came back he was fully committed to *Step* and said,

> 'Christian literature must look as attractive as secular literature, must hold its own on the news stands in the street, and must be capable of selling in the commercial market.'

The content had to be good too — the subject matter and the quality of writing. It had to begin where young people were and not where 'Christian dog-collars' thought they ought to be.

It tackled live issues. Why, for example, were young African men choosing not to marry until they were in their thirties? Why so much hypocrisy in funeral orations? How long were children expected to go on 'obeying their parents' as it said in the Bible? How were young Christians to respond to gossip, or birth control or treatment of servants? And what struggles would you have to go through if you wanted to find a meaningful life?

Step proved popular in Kenya, Nigeria, Uganda, Zambia and Zimbabwe and has made its most recent appearance in French in Burkino Faso. Hopefully this is the beginning of a wider service for Francophone Africa.

Meanwhile, our visionary moved on, until at one point his journalism led him into such fiercely Christian criticism of the government that he was sentenced to a term of imprisonment in one of the major Kenyan crackdowns on opposition. But he went on and so did his vision. And by that time others had caught it and begun to have visions of their own.

TORTURED FOR TRUTH

A Methodist Superintendent in the Philippines with a flair for asking awkward questions

Nonoy (Toribio Cajiuat) is one of twenty Methodist Superintendents in the Philippines. He has a flair for asking awkward questions and challenging authority, especially when he sees the sufferings inflicted on his country by colonialism and the sufferings inflicted on the poor by the well-to-do. In a more democratic society he may hardly be noticed. Too many others would be saying the same things.

In the Philippines it is different. Methodist Supers are expected to carry out the orders of the Bishop, care for the faithful who keep the churches going and attend to administration. To a degree Toribio does all three (though not unquestioningly!) but his real commitment is to poor farmers and fisherfolk who in the struggle for survival need help.

It was for their sakes that after three years of study in the United States, where everyone expected him to settle, he felt the call to come back home. Toribio's gospel must be good news for them and he preaches it not only in the pulpit but also in the fields and by the seaside as he helps the poorest to organize fishery projects and rural community programmes.

Small wonder that with martial law under Marcos he was arrested as a subversive and charged with being a communist. For three days he was kept without food and then brought out naked, handcuffed to two filing cabinets, and questioned by three senior officers.

When he failed to satisfy them with his answers the heavy mob were brought in who treated him to rifle butts all over his body. (Women, he says, suffered far more!) He was then returned to his cell and the process was repeated every day for a fortnight, after which he was sent to a concentration camp.

For six months his wife, Purita ('My ministry would be lame without her'), held down her job as a teacher, cared for two young children, ran his church as a pastor, visited him in prison and spent her evenings going to one authoriity after another to secure his release. After six months, and thanks to the pressure of the international Christian community, he was set free and allowed to continue his ministry.

> I used to think I was poor. Then they told me I wasn't poor, I was needy. Then they told me it was self-defeating to think of myself as needy, I was deprived. Then they told me deprived was a bad image. I was under-privileged. Then they told me under-privileged was over-used. I was disadvantaged. I still don't have a cent. But I have a great vocabulary. [5.4]

STRUGGLING TO STAND

Some people are just determined to get up and walk

In Zimbabwe . . .

In the late 1980s the Adult Literacy Organization of Zimbabwe had over 100 literacy teachers, all of whom needed a mini-library and a regular supply of newspapers and magazines which could be used for teaching purposes.

They also had nearly as many teaching centres, each of which needed a local reading room, if not a library. For security reasons it needed to be housed in a local school or church, and whichever provided the service was liable itself to benefit also, though it always had to be clear that all the community must have access to it.

It was also important for new readers to have something of their own. One copy going through dozens of hands is hardly satisfactory.

. . . and in Russia

In 1992, *Christian Times*, an eight-page Baptist newspaper in full colour, had a circulation of 50,000. Because Russian families are large they reckoned it was read by 200,000.

'If only every reader could pay for it', said the editor! The most anyone could afford was the price of a coffee, about one-third of what it cost even with a print run of 50,000. What was worse, he was expected every month to place free copies in libraries, homes for the elderly and prisons.

Fortunately he had a sense of humour! He chuckled over one letter from a prisoner who asked for a *second free* copy because by the time he got the first it had passed through so many hands that all the ink had worn off. Hope in the darkness!

WHY CANNOT THESE PEOPLE MAKE A LIVING?

Because land — the equivalent of wealth in a developed country — is concentrated in so few hands. In South America, overall, 17% of the landowners control 90% of the land. . . . over a third of the rural population must make do with just *1% of the cropland*; in Africa, three-quarters of the people have access to not quite 4% of the land. World Bank figures for twenty two under- developed countries show that on average, fully a third of the 'active agricultural population' has *no land at all*.

There is also another vitally important factor in keeping poor people hungry for which the developed countries cannot shirk responsibility . . . all of us in the developed countries profit from it to the degree that Third World people are subsidizing our breakfasts, lunches, dinners, underwear, shirts, sheets, automobile tyres, etc, etc through their cheap labour. This factor is the so called 'cash crop' that demands so much time, space and effort in the poor countries. [5.5]

THE CUTTING EDGE

ALFALIT began as a missionary literacy operation from Florida in the 1960s, though how much it was committed to literacy *per se* or to literacy as a means of making converts depends to some extent on who you talk to. By the mid-1980s, however, it was clear. The break with Florida had come and ALFALIT became an indigenous Latin American organization, with headquarters in Costa Rica and programmes in seventeen countries.

The nature of the work also changed. It began to see itself as an educational programme and agent of change within Latin American society. It began to describe itself as 'a Christian community for human development in Latin America' directed at 'the marginal people' whose aim is 'to encourage self-development in the communities' and 'to enable those communities to discover that they can find solutions to their own problems by taking concrete action'.

The concern for literacy was not lost but now formed one of eight programmes, the other seven being adult basic education, disaster relief, advancement of women, literature production, helping marginal people to improve their economy, simple health education for health workers and training church workers to be agents of change within their own communities.

ALFALIT's churchmanship is very wide and they claim connections with over 1,000 local churches representing 150 denominations, many of them Pentecostal.

From being a straightforward mission agency or literacy organization ALFALIT has become an agent of change through literacy and literature.

THE CHANGING FACE

The **Christian University in Tomahon,** Sulawesi (Indonesia) is five hours by air from Jakarta and thirty miles up in the mountains. It caters only for the Presbyterian Church in the Minahassa tribes who are only found in the very small tip at the north end of the island. But this should not give the impression that it is a miniature affair. Far from it!

Founded as a Faculty of Theology in 1962, it now has five other Faculties, 1500 theological students (700 taking BD) and some 40 faculty, 25 of them full-time and 14 currently away studying at other universities in order to continue their own education. The library has around 14,000 books, 85% in English, and the School has an excellent Statement of Goals for the Library, complete with explanatory notes.

The Presbyterian Seminary in Tobelo, Halmahera, one of the 'spice islands', is totally different and even more remote.

200 students recently moved here from Ternate to be more at the heart of their church life and have been busy constructing a new campus. They have a Faculty of twenty three, sixteen of whom are part-time, and a library of some 4,000 titles, mostly English and more the result of freewill offerings than planned growth.

Down the road there is a Rural Development Centre where students and church members work side by side in various forms of manual activity, including constructing beds and keeping rabbits, hens and pigs as a means of developing agriculture and relating theology to life.

Widows at the Cross

The women who attended Jesus at the cross may not literally have been widows, but they shared a sense of loss. One whom they loved had died, and when they went to pay their respects on the Sunday morning the body had 'disappeared'.

Read Mark 15: 40-7 and 16: 1-8 (with parallel passages in Matthew and Luke) and before hastening to the joys of the resurrection take time to appreciate the sense of loss with which Easter Day began. Relate the experiences of the women to those of the Widows of Chile referred to in Lent.

In that way the story may speak to many people who have difficulty with the more familiar Easter story because it rehearses events so far away, or who have heard it so often that it fails to come fresh.

Explore Easter as the violence that crucifies the innocent and, picking up from Lent, provides the summons to make a choice. But then use *Widows* to demonstrate how not everyone believes it or even wants to believe it.

The New Testament story is about the crucifiers, the crucified and the women. *Widows* is about the Green, the Dust and the Old Woman.

The Green is an alliance of the landowner, the military and a young man who knows which side his bread is buttered. They have ruled for generations. Their land is fertile. They have a vested interest in maintaining *status quo*. So hush things up, calm things down, pretend nothing ever happened and look to the future.

The Dust are the peasants. There is much in the lifestyle of the Green which they covet, but if they ever 'get ideas', or dare to lay claim to it, 'everything decent, beautiful and civilized gets covered in dust'. These are the men whose bodies have been bruised, beaten and killed (the 'disappeared') and the women who loved them and find it hard to believe that they will never come back.

The Old Woman is the grandmother who refuses to let go, who sits by the river and waits. She pleads with her family to keep up the struggle, with the river to give up its dead and (when it does) with the military to allow her to give her husband a decent burial.

Explore the arguments for doing nothing. What we are dealing with is mindless, unresisted violence which leads to death — but from the point of view of the Green it is the stupid and pointless death of people who didn't really matter very much anyway and would soon be forgotten if only you could keep the lid on long enough. The arguments are all too familiar. Of course things had gone wrong. Of course what had happened never should have happened. But you can't live there for ever. Life must go on. And that means forgetting and adjusting. Picking up the pieces. In any case, now it's all over. People soon forget. The media will lose interest.

The only problem is a bunch of crazy women. They may be afraid, but they could be dangerous. They just can't or won't accept what has happened. They seem determined to keep something alive.

From their point of view, of course, it looks different, but then are they to compound stupidity by raising their heads above the parapet and going the same way or are they to keep their heads down, soothe their brow with platitudes and wait for better times? The choice is a hard one. Only one seems ready to make it. She waits for the dead to return, and if he does not return alive then she wants his body for a proper burial.

And she it is who provides the pointer to the resurrection. Such is her conviction that she even refuses to save her grandson, though not without at the same time giving him the courage to take the bullets and explaining why he too must die: so that truth and right can be established and future generations can be told of what he did, the stand he took, the price he paid, and derive strength from it.

Strength in Weakness

Begin with Paul's comments on wisdom and foolishness (I Cor 1: 18-31) and his response to 'the thorn in the flesh' (II Cor 12: 10). Relate this on the one hand to the crucifixion and on the other to some of the human situations, particularly in the developing world, where what passes for weakness turns out to be strength.

Paint a picture of a young boy, small of stature, low on muscle and a prey to bullying. Show how he uses other skills, his wits, his tongue, his charm or whatever, so as to demonstrate the strength of weakness.

From there cite other instances which challenge the assumption that might is right. Nurses, for example, have a strength in society out of all proportion to their physical force or their salaries, as any government, however large its majority, usually finds once it takes them on. Find other examples from contemporary events.

Explore the power of music to rouse, to inspire or to comfort, the power of conviction which enables people to spend years in prison rather than surrender, and the power of laughter to transform a situation, as for example when the victims going to the gas chambers took it upon themselves to laugh at their captors.

Consider why things that look mighty and powerful are so easily threatened by things that look weak. The elephant afraid of the mouse! Why? Or the tactics which the powerful employ, like despising the things and the people that you can't handle. Naaman did it with the Jordan. It was a mere trickle, a dirty little stream! Were not Abana and Pharpar, rivers of Damascus, better than all the waters of Israel? But they weren't! And Naaman had to come to terms with it (II Kings 5).

But perhaps in that story we have a clue. Real strength is not shouting, fighting and winning. Real strength is in yielding and being healed.

Western agencies and governments, committed to Western capitalism, find it hard to accept this. We so readily assume that big schemes, big projects, big agencies and big money will provide the answers, when often what is needed is something small and simple. A good water supply for a village which works is better than a big dam which creates problems.

Rural farmers may have been dismissed by the West as weak and ignorant by the big guns of colonialism who knew better, but history and experience often demonstrate that the local people know best what will work for them.

The troubles arise when the weak feel they have to ape the strong, and they do. Unarmed nations want arms. Non-nuclear powers want nuclear weapons. Rural countries want industry. Minority churches, created in many cases to challenge the Establishment, want recognition. So that instead of demonstrating strength in our weakness we too often parade our weakness in our search for strength.

Children are wiser. One they know their weakness and their inability to compete they very often find a satisfactory alternative way forward. In their weakness they become strong, and the most disruptive force in any family is the baby.

AVOID THE BIG PROJECT

Colonialism and the dependency syndrome major on second-rate people and engender subservience rather than creativity. One solution is to tap the best resources in the country and avoid big projects which are more likely to line the pockets of politicians or people in the donor countries than to provide any kind of trickle-down effect for Africa.

— Zimbabwe Christian Leader

Things to Do

NO BUS COMING

A bus full of local people is winding its way through the tropical rain forest, somewhere in Africa, Asia or South America, when all at once the engine fails and everything comes to a halt.

The driver and a few of the more knowledgeable passengers apply the usual treatment. Nothing happens. Someone with a mobile phone tries to call for help. There is no connection. They wait for someone else to come along. Nobody does.

Obviously they are going to have to wait until the next bus comes twenty four hours later, which as likely as not will be full anyway. It never comes.

Slowly the truth dawns — there is no bus coming. No help, no emergency services, no delivery. They are on their own!

Try to enter into their situation by recalling occasions when you have been desperate and had to call for help, e.g. a car breakdown, an accident in the home, a sudden illness. Recall how you felt, how the situation was resolved and what you might have done if no help had come.

Go out of your way for a month to find stories like that by reading the papers, talking to friends, etc. Make a list and then analyse them to see how they are alike and how they differ.

Read the biography of someone who was held hostage. How did they cope?

Widen it to a community. eg the isolation of the mining communities and others like them. Reflect again on communities like Aberfan, Hungerford and Dunblane, and distinguish between the help they received and the experience where no help could be given.

Relate their stories to those of the developing world — alone, yet with extraordinary resources.

THE QUEEN CAME BY

Programme notes at a recent production of **The Queen Came By** (Delderfield) pointed out that to celebrate Queen Victoria's Diamond Jubilee London spent a quarter of a million pounds on street decorations. On the banqueting table, 60,000 orchids from all over the empire, and 2,500 beacons blazing all over the country.

All the traditional Victorian values were there: the Queen and the empire, the Union Jack and the Royal Navy, the music hall and the chorus girls. But so too were all the evils of the same period that Dickens wrote about: long working hours, poor living conditions, low wages, orphans, illness and the exploitation of women, the Irish question, dirt, grime and squalor.

When Victoria died three and a half years later a novelist wrote, 'The Queen was a most mischievous fetish for a most hypocritical nation. Her influence on society was nil; she did not even know what society had become. She never entered it . . .'

No! She only came by.

Choose a topic (land, hunger, literature, etc) and invite three people (or groups) to explore it in terms of Victorian times in Britain, today in Britain and the developing nations today. Invite a fourth person to explore the topic in biblical terms. Discuss.

List the similarities and differences, with special attention to the reactions of society. Classify the reactions (indifferent, patronizing, accusatory, compassionate, etc.) and discuss the similarities and differences.

Write down (privately) what reactions you would like to have and what you do have. Discuss as fully as you feel able.

Introduce the biblical element. What difference does it make to your reactions and to your understanding of the Bible?

Finally, try to settle for one thing you can do, individually or together, to change things.

Food for Thought
— Food for Prayer

WRITERS' WORKSHOPS

Anyone who has difficulty writing a letter will know something of the problems of writing. It is often assumed that established writers have no difficulty but that is not true. When John Steinbeck wrote *East of Eden* he set himself so many words a day, but to get himself going he started each day by writing a letter to his publishers, sometimes setting out what he was going to say and sometimes just to get himself going at all. Another established writer said she could only achieve it if she took good care first thing in the morning never to begin doing anything else, not even answering the post.

In some developing countries Writers' Workshops have proved a helpful way of overcoming these obstacles. They cannot exactly teach people to write, but they can help them to get going so that their natural talent flows.

Sometimes publishers find a Writers' Workshop a useful way of recruiting and training writers. Bedan Mbugwa's *Step* in Kenya was particularly good at it and ISPCK (India) run workshops at national level where established authors share their expertise with budding writers anxious to use their skill to change social thinking.

Imagine a Saturday afternoon. A dozen people, with writing potential but limited experience, have been brought together for a couple of sessions. Each was told to bring 'a story' which could be read in not more than five minutes. After each has read their story the leader asks three simple questions:

1 What was good about it?

2 What was bad about it?

3 What could be done to improve it?

Beginnings and endings proved critical. So did length of sentences, choice of words, attention to detail, the distinction between conveying ideas and evoking feelings, being didactic and being open, and so on. They learned from one another, sometimes spotting their own weaknesses in somebody else's script without anybody saying a word.

Pray for

— people who want to write but have difficulty

— people who are trying to find simple and painless ways of helping them

— editors looking for new writers

— readers who are looking for writers with something to say and an ability to say it simply and well.

LEARNING ENGLISH

1 Imagine reading a specialist book on any subject. Think about the difficulties posed by the language, the sentence construction, the ideas, etc. Reflect on the difficulty you sometimes have when it comes to reading the small print of an agreement or detailed instructions for handling your new video, etc.

2 Imagine having to do the same operations in a second language. Consider carefully the difference between this experience and 'getting by' in French or conversational German.

3 Imagine a visit to a library where 85% of the books are in your second language, and the rest mainly English with a smattering of Welsh and Gaelic.

4 Try to enter into the experience of many people round the world who have to master the niceties of English before they can really get to grips with biblical and theological study.

Learning English to study theology is no longer a luxury — it's a necessity!

For Confession

Reflect on the way we make judgments, sometimes moral, sometimes Christian and sometimes simply according to Western standards, and acknowledge our failure so often

— to see people

— to appreciate them for their character and skills

— to wonder at, and to rejoice with them, in the remarkable things they can do

— to seek judgments that will benefit them rather than please us.

For Thanksgiving

Identify and specify some of the riches in other nations, races and religions and be thankful for the way in which they can enich our lives.

For Others

Pray for those people who in the estimation of others 'have arrived' and can 'walk tall', remembering that that is not always how they see themselves

— the rich person who feels people think that all he or she has to offer is money

— the professional person who feels he or she is only wanted for their technical expertise

— the people at the bottom who feel nobody ever thinks they have anything to give

— many in the developing nations who feel 'hurt' because the West seems uninterested in what they have to offer.

Category

Music and Cassettes, Posters and Pictures

Remember

Composers, arrangers, recording technicians, artists and painters

Focus On

a piece of music, poster or picture which 'spoke volumes' to you, and still does. Give thanks for what it says and for those who created it

---

LITERATURE, QUEEN OF THE PROJECTS

Primary attention is now being given to basic needs (à la Freire) and from there they go on to reading. The change began in 1985. The old-style approach was to teach people to read and to get them involved in projects. What teachers found was that this really made evaluation impossible. They now find that by attacking projects such as food, health, clothing, etc they can evaluate what happens and relate this to patterns of reading.

One three-year plan has four programmes plus one that relates to them all. The four programmes are for women, literacy, the communities and the churches. The production of literature is the fifth which relates to them all.

Pray for Booksellers

who have to balance the stock they would like to carry

with the cash they have and the books they can confidently sell

EASTER TO PENTECOST
A Time for Vision

Theme

There stood beside them two men, robed in white, who said, 'Men of
Galilee, why stand you there looking up into the sky?'

Acts 1: 11 (REB)

If we have problems with Easter, how can we possibly cope with the ascension? And how do we handle the adjustments called for by the sudden changes: first, a suffering Messiah, then a dying Lord, then a risen Saviour, an empty tomb, and now an ascension?

'Two men, robed in white' suggest that instead of looking upward to where he has gone, we might try looking around to see where he is. Not out there, but here among. Not backwards, but forwards. Not Jerusalem, but Galilee. Not where you would naturally expect, but where you might easily miss.

What the ascension provides is a watershed — a double watershed, in fact.

One, between the world as it was (Jerusalem with all its structure and security) and the world as it is going to be (the wide open spaces of Galilee).

The other, between dependence on the physical presence of Jesus, and learning to go on their own, to find their way, create their own vision, accept responsibility for their own decisions; learning to balance the thrill and satisfaction of getting it right with the frustrations and disappointments (not to mention the guilt) when it turns out wrong.

Ascension begins a quest for a living Christ, present every bit as much as before but in a different way, and for a God who had demonstrated his power in exodus and exile but who would not necessarily do so in the same way in the future. It meant learning to look in different places, recognize different signs, and make connections.

The disciples had already made the break. There was certainly no going back! But the road ahead still called for much adjustment as each new twist challenged their understanding and tested their faith. Each moment of emotional enthusiasm was checked by reason and understanding. Each step their head moved forward, their heart was slow to catch up, and sometimes missed a beat.

Like the disciples, many people in the developing world have discovered what happens when you take the ascension seriously.

key word	Ascension marks the final appearance of Jesus in bodily form. What happened or what it meant we cannot know. The NT is careful not to tell us. The Greek simply says he was 'carried away' (Luke 24: 51) or 'lifted up' (Acts 1: 9), but from now on he is 'not here'. From now on we must learn to meet him in a fresh place and in a new way.
Ascension	

The Poor

What they Know and What they Want

To think of the poor simply as people lacking in money and resources is not even half-a-truth! It is a sad reflection on a way of life which judges everything in terms of numbers, cash and the economy. When extreme famine, drought or earthquake devastate your land little imagination is needed to appreciate what it means to have friends.

For the rest of the time, however, very few of us want well-meaning neighbours and relatives moving in, even with the best of intentions, to take over our lives. Yet for the world's poor, and especially for the poor nations, this distinction is not always an option.

This helps to explain why the developing nations bitterly resent the way in which their real problems are too often clouded by the West's preoccupation with aid, projects, disaster and development, not to mention their own internal politics.

What they know

They know that much overseas aid is motivated more by a desire to help those providing it than those receiving it and that, though urban poverty may be their major problem and represent what most deprives them of their dignity, Western fund-raising methods are more likely to be effective if they portray mud huts and not cities.

They know that where resources are lacking it is often because such resources as they had have been taken away from them, often by the very nations which now are falling over themselves to help — a variation perhaps on selling arms to your enemies and then expressing horror when they are used against you!

They know that big money and big schemes are rarely the solution to their problems and that intermediate technology and simple, locally-inspired changes can bring considerable transformation, but they also know that we in the West are still sure that *their* salvation lies down *our* road.

They know that even in the best of societies big money brings with it its own corruption. They also know how often it corrupts those who handle it as well.

They know the resources they have which are under-developed. As Dominique Lapierre demonstrates in *The City of Joy*, poor people have enormous personal resources for coping with problems, even disasters, which helpful Western aid agency workers could scarcely begin to understand. Were that not so they would have expired long since.

But the resources which they have are often not the sort Western nations most want to hear about. It is much easier to respond to distress than it is gently and lovingly to nurture resourcefulness. It is also more immediately satisfying, makes better news stories, raises more money and doesn't take nearly as long.

They know that the nations and agencies which are most generous with advice are very often the ones which find it most difficult to address those very same problems in their own country.

But if the problems the agencies face in their own countries can only be addressed by changing government policy and social attitudes, what leads them to believe that it might be any different in developing countries?

What they want

At rock bottom, they want dignity, equality, collegiality, mutuality, fraternity, and a recognition that none of us lives in a world where the idea that some nations are rich and other nations are poor is taken for granted as inevitable. Some of them would prefer to think that even given the wide variation in basic resources we are all both rich and poor at the same time only in different ways, and that all the resources belong to God.

Perhaps the place to start is with the 'rich nations' identifying their own poverty (which is not economic) and then beginning to work out fresh patterns of sharing so that instead of givers and receivers (or, even worse, donors and receivers) we all begin to give and receive {different gifts and resources) from one another.

A first step would be a recognition that the poor exist as people, in contrast to the tendency to turn them into an underclass we don't even see. If we are compelled to see them, we don't hear them. And if we are compelled to hear them, we have our own devices for not listening. They know what they want to tell us — they also know it is no use.

In London, New York, Singapore, Hong Kong and many cities of Europe, listening means literally bringing the poor out of their ghettos (or shop doorways!) and working out patterns of new life.

In Australia, as John Pilger points out in *A Secret Country* where he makes comparisons between white attitudes to the Aborigines of Australia and the blacks of South Africa, it means coming to terms with history. The past cannot be re-written, but a recognition of the past could at least be the first step towards confession and repentance, towards forgiveness and re-alignment.

A second step might be to stop using the Bible and religion to bolster up the theories, ideas and attitudes which, however attractive they may be to some, can have no place in a truly biblical and Christian theology.

Ceresko, for example, in *Introduction to the Old Testament. A Liberation Perspective* (pp. 3-4), reminds us how for years Dutch Reformed theologians drew upon the traditions of the exodus from Egypt as a prototype of the experience of the Boers, whom they saw as escaping from the slavery imposed by British colonialism in the Cape and then subordinating the indigenous populations of the Orange Free State because they regarded them as the Canaanites whom God had ordered them to destroy or subdue. Then, with a different but no more acceptable 'twist', Ceresko shows how the indigenous people found their own mandate in the same story of the exodus and used it in the struggle for a free and better world.

One of the reasons some people have difficulty appreciating the Easter message of the resurrection is that they have such fixed ideas as to what it is. So they look but rarely find. Perhaps, like the early disciples, they are looking in the wrong place — Jerusalem rather than Galilee. And if we cannot appreciate the resurrection among the poor ('making to stand up', 'making to rise and leave their place', 'awakening' or even 'rising up') and our calling to participate in it we could be doing the same. Looking in a different place may be part of it. Asking a different set of questions may be another. [6.1]

Do not attempt to do us any more good. Your good has done us too much harm already

(Egyptian Sheik in London, 1884)

TO BUILD SOMETHING TOGETHER
among the Poor of Calcutta

Dominique Lapierre's hero in The City of Joy *is Kovalski, a Polish Roman priest who goes to Calcutta not to exercise a Christian ministry, like Mother Teresa, but simply to get away from Poland after the death of his father and 'to achieve by other means what previously he had attempted to do by violence'. In Calcutta he hears voices he has never heard before and when he tries to build what the people want he is surprised by their choice.*

'In these slums, people actually put love and mutual support into practice. They know how to be tolerant of all creeds and castes, how to give respect to a stranger, how to show charity towards beggars, cripples, lepers and even the insane. Here the weak were helped, not trampled upon. Orphans were instantly adopted by their neighbours and old people were cared for and revered by their children.'

THE CURSE OF DEPENDENCY

'Help serves only to make people more dependent *unless it is supported with actions designed to wipe out the actual roots of poverty.*

Does that mean that it's no use taking them out of their hovels full of crap and setting them up in new housing?

Max nodded his head sadly . . . .

"In a slum an exploiter is better than a Santa Claus . . . an exploiter forces you to react, whereas a Santa Claus immobilizes you".' [6.2]

'A blind man of about thirty was squatting at the end of the main street in front of a small boy struck down with polio. He was speaking to the boy as he gently massaged first the youngster's needle-thin calves, then his deformed knees and thighs. The boy held on to the man's neck with a look overcome with gratitude. His blind companion was laughing. He was still so young, yet he exuded a serenity and goodness that was almost supernatural.

After a few minutes he stood up and took the boy delicately by the shoulders to get him on his feet. The latter made an effort to support himself on his legs. The blind man spoke a few words and the lad put one foot in front of him into the murky water that swamped the street. Again the blind man pushed him gently forward and the child moved his other leg. He had taken a step.

Reassured, he took a second. After a few minutes they both were making their way down the middle of the alley, the little boy acting as guide for his brother in darkness and the latter propelling the young polio victim forward. So remarkable was the sight of those two castaways that even the children playing marbles on the kerbstones stood up to watch as they passed.' [6.3]

NOBODY KNOWS
AND NOBODY WANTS TO KNOW

'At the 1988 Remembrance Day service in Sydney an Aboriginal man attempted to place flowers on the Cenotaph during the playing of the Last Post. He was stopped and led away. "I have a right to lay a wreath for my people", he said; "I represent the Aborigines who died defending their land, *our* land".'

The Aborigines in Australia have no rights. Not even the rights of the Indians in North America or the Maoris in New Zealand. What is worse, nobody knows the story, nobody wants to know, and if somebody tries to tell it nobody wants to listen.

When John Pilger wrote about it in the press one journalist phoned to ask if he was serious. He'd known all about it for years but he never wrote about it.

Why?

'Because they were only coons and lived like animals' and anyway 'nobody gives a damn'.

John Pilger, who tells the story in *A Secret Country*, continues,

'In South Africa I was greeted warmly by white people, mostly of English origin, who spoke about "good old Aussie" and cricket and beer drinking. They alluded cautiously, wistfully, to a land without blacks. What they meant was a land with perfect blacks — blacks who were there but who were reckoned not to be there.

These English South Africans believed themselves to be liberal people, proud of their distinction from the "uncivilized" Afrikaners on the veldt, bull-whips behind their backs. Most of these liberal people had not seen, or had not wished to see, the fringes of their own towns and cities, where people lived in cardboard houses without running water and behind barbed wire and watchtowers.' [6.4]

THREE TYPES OF DONOR

1 The 'missionary' who wants to help uplift an under-privileged community. 'They could do it just as well in their own country but they want to work in the Third World.'

2 People who cannot make the grade in their own country, go overseas and masquerade as 'do-gooders'. Their main motive is self-satisfaction and they spoil the work of the first group.

3 People who like to come on two- to three-year work permits (believing Zimbabwe to be God's own country) to help train local personnel but who quickly discover a strong white community and gravitate to it. They then find themselves indoctrinated by those whites who still believe a black man cannot do a job as well as a white one and their confidence is undermined. The result is that they extend their contracts and work mainly with second-rate blacks, who of course make mistakes and so fulfil the expectations of their teachers. All this is still colonialism and the dependency syndrome in a new guise. [6.5]

LIBRARIES IN ALL SHAPES AND SIZES

It is a warm Sunday afternoon in Kitwe, on the Copperbelt, in Zambia. Two boys, aged about nine and eleven, are wandering barefoot along a dusty track not far from the Mindolo Ecumenical Foundation, a centre for all kinds of Christian agencies including the YWCA, a literature centre, a theological college, a bookroom and the splendid Dag Hammarskjöld library.

With hands behind their backs, each has a book. Minutes later they are lying on the floor with a dozen or so African friends of the same age, all reading. On a day and at a time when many libraries in the West would be closed these youngsters are making full use of their birthright.

In Mathare Valley, Nairobi, an area of extreme poverty and degradation, comparable perhaps to Harlem in New York in the 1960s, you may be hard pressed to find a library at all. But they do exist. They are being created all the time, though some of them may not survive very long. They are often called mini-libraries because that is exactly what they are — small collections of books, and nothing more.

They may be in a church hall, or a health centre or a school. As likely as not, they will have been put there by the Sisters of St Paul. Mostly they will be kept under lock and key, not necessarily because the Valley boasts so many thieves (though it probably does, as do most communities which have to live in extreme poverty) but because in spite of their poverty these are the communities where books are treasured. And what happens in Mathare Valley is happening in various ways in many other parts of Africa and Asia.

In the Sudan they used to be called Shoebox Libraries, the brainchild of Joyce Chaplin, *(Writers, My Friends*, David C. Cook Foundation, 1984, p 58.). That started one morning when a man from Malawi received a consignment of books to lend to his friends and in the kitchen, where he spent most of his time, all he could find to keep them 'nice' was a shoebox. So he called it his Shoebox Library.

One of Joyce's helpers at that time was Martha Mandao. As a result of watching her friends closely Martha noticed that people had different motives for reading. She began to identify different readership groups, each with its own needs and interests. She lent books in English and Swahili. She got a thrill from watching people read and finding it profitable, and as the number of Shoeboxes grew she it was who came up with the Shoebox Library motto: 'The right book for the right person'.

The variety of books was very wide: health, nutrition, economics, agriculture, literacy, education and, of course, Christian affairs. The libraries met more than a reading need. As people shared books they shared ideas, vision and enthusiasm. And from Sudan they spread to Francophone Africa, Ghana, Nigeria, Kenya, Uganda, Zambia, Egypt, India, Bangladesh, Philippines, Papua New Guinea, and even to the UK.

In South America, where floor space was at a premium, many women developed a pattern of Wall Libraries — a huge piece of tough material on to which women had sewn a dozen pockets, each of which held one book on full display. Sometimes they were hung in public places and served as a lending library.

Often Wall Libraries were a crucial part of literacy programmes. You were given one when you reached a certain stage in the learning process. It hung on your wall like a Diploma or Certificate, the only difference being that before you were given it you had to give an undertaking to teach someone else to read.

RE IN SCHOOLS
NOT ONLY A PROBLEM OF MONEY

Books for schools are a problem everywhere. In developing countries it is at its most difficult. When it comes to Religious Education the temptation for most governments is simply to expect the churches to povide. Yet all the churches have limited resources and many have none at all. In Hungary in the late 1980s it produced special problems

The problem of providing literature in developing or poorer countries is not always a matter of literacy or personal poverty. Sometimes it is the poverty of the institution, sometimes inflation, sometimes the economy, sometimes just foreign exchange.

When Hungary became independent in the late 1980s there were reported to be some 400 publishing houses in the country, 50 state-owned and the rest private. They had an annual turnover of £20,000,000, an official inflation rate of 36% and a real inflation rate nearer 50%. Books had to be produced and sold against a tight economic background.

The average salary was just over £100 per month, the minimum about £50. But there were well in excess of 100,000 people, mainly business folk, whose minimum monthly income was somewhere between £4,000-7,000. Highest incomes among the educated went to the lawyers, financial experts, doctors and vets, down to an average monthly income of around £150.

Producing books for the churches and schools in that climate was a problem. The Reformed Church (the dominant Protestant Church) was commissioned by the government to provide for the needs of RE but not given any money to do it. Nor was money the only problem.

What were they to produce? With the exception of a few church schools there had been no religious education in the schools of Hungary for forty years.

Few teachers had either training or experience. The sort of debates which we take for granted on RE teaching content and method were unknown.

There was plenty of material in English and some samples were actually sent, but of course they were totally unsuitable for the Hungarian situation. The most they could hope to do was to give ideas and stimulate local production.

But then who was to read them, evaluate them for Hungary and set up any kind of publishing programme? Few with any skill in RE could read English. Few who could read English had any skill in RE. Fewer still had the capacity to write.

In the end the burden fell on one man, Kalman Tarr, head of the Publishing House of the Reformed Church, who carried many other major responsibilities, to read, evaluate, plan, engage writers and publish.

Yet within a couple of years, financed by literature agencies outside Hungary, the church was producing textbooks for all ages. Editions of 20,000 were sold immediately with reprints of the same number out of stock within another two years. Two books for beginners were followed by two for middle schools.

As other countries opened up, the market went far beyond Hungary to other Hungarian-speaking groups in places as far apart as Transylvania and the Ukraine, few of whom had any possibility of paying for them.

TALKING DRUMS

John Carrington was a young Baptist missionary in what was then the Belgian Congo. On one occasion, when he and a senior colleague were out visiting forest villages, they suddenly decided to pop over to the nearest town some seven or eight miles away.

On arrival they found the village teacher, doctor and church members all waiting for them in the schoolroom. No message had been sent, as far as they knew, and indeed no messenger could have got there before them. So how did they know they were coming? Answer: the drum message.

Carrington's interest was sufficiently aroused for him to make it the subject of a thesis for which he got a doctorate, and the story was popularized in *The Talking Drums of Africa.*

His first discovery was that the drum message was no ordinary drum beat. This was not just a noise saying, 'Look out! There's an enemy on the way,' which could be varied by a different kind of noise saying, ' Friends are coming. Get out the best china!' It was 'a beat which spoke'.

He then discovered that in Africa this was commonplace. More than a hundred years ago a traveller reported that the Africans had 'a system of communication' which we now know was in some respects as effective as our phone or radio. There is a story from 1881 of a wrecked steamer which was reported sixty to seventy miles away within a couple of hours — and not just the fact, but the details — because a good drummer can say almost anything he wants to say on his drums.

What the African teaches us is that there are different ways of hearing and it is not easy for the European to understand because it is something to do with tone.

For example, there are at least six different messages you can convey through the same three words ('he went outside') according to your tone.

he went outside (she didn't)

he went *out*side (not inside)

he went *outside*? (in this weather?)

he *went* outside (but I don't know where he is now)

he went *out*side (why don't you listen?)

he went-outside! (I don't believe it!)

Similarly, we are familiar with the way different people hear different sounds. A child gets a drum for Christmas, By Boxing Day he is driving his mother wild. 'For goodness sake, stop that noise!' she yells; 'you're driving me crazy!' 'But mum,' he responds, ' I'm leading the soldiers down the Mall for the Changing of the Guard.' She hears one sound (a noise); he hears another (music).

And different people here the same sounds differently. Two children are whisked out of the gunfire of Sarajevo, Uganda or Indonesia to safety in London. They arrive on November 2 and breathe peacefully in their beds at night for the first time for months. Then on the 5th November the younger one wakes up terrified. They're back in the firing line! The older one wakes up and smiles. He's heard about fireworks. Same noise. Different sound.

What Carrington realized was that when the African heard a drum he heard something different from the European and so he set about learning the language.

But today there are more Africans who can handle the phone and the fax than Europeans who can appreciate the talking drums. [6.6]

THE CUTTING EDGE

New Day, Philippines, is a publishing house established by the churches in Manila as an independent charitable foundation with its own board.

Gloria Rodriguez became editor in the early 1970s, came to Oxford for training as a Feed the Minds scholar in 1977, and recently retired as Director, leaving a healthy and self-sufficient Christian publishing house for her successor, Beatriz Bautista.

After depending in its early days on grants and subsidies New Day now covers normal running costs, though capital expenditure for large items like a van, computer or warehouse can still present problems.

They publish about forty titles a year and reprint a further twenty five, plus six issues of *Upper Room* in English and three other languages.

Suriyaban Publishers, Bangkok, is the publishing house of the Church of Christ in Thailand, which owes its origins to Presbyterian missionaries from the USA and British missionaries coming over from China as early as 1828. In its present form it goes back to 1934 and today represents about half the Protestants in the country with a membership of 65,000. It stands firmly in the Reformed tradition

There are eight different departments, one of which is committed to Christian education and literature, from which the Suriyaban Publishers sprang in 1960. Besides publishing they have three book shops, two of them in Bangkok.

'Suriya' means sun, and 'ban' means literature, so a rough translation may be 'Literature of the Light'. Since, in Thai, the sun is also the symbol for God, an alternative might be 'God's Word'.

THE CHANGING FACE

The Interdenominational Theological Seminary of Theology (SEIT) began in the late 1970s to train pastors for the Northern Zone of Buenos Aires. With the growth of the Argentine Missionary Movement, it developed a vision for training cross-cultural missionaries alongside pastoral training. Currently it provides a holistic (theological/cross-cultural) missionary and pastoral training. There are four emphases.

1 Academic. It aims to raise academic standards and to achieve recognition through AETAL, a Latin American accreditation body.

2 Spiritual. Weekly worship groups concentrate on discipleship prayer and reflection.

3 Practical. All students are expected to be active in their local churches. Students on degree level missionary courses must do a year of cross-cultural practical experience after the first two years of their training.

4 'Filials'. Centres of training based in local churches, related to the seminary, for local people. In a city as big as Buenos Aires it makes more sense for one teacher rather than twelve students to cross the city!

SEIT is an institution with many opportunities but is still struggling with inadequate premises and a restricted library. It is committed to training people who will serve the whole church, sharing the whole gospel with the whole world.

Going Away

Begin by reflecting on the way books and papers are taken for granted in Western society. In your mind's eye, go through each room of your house and think about the literature you have there. Consider how many newspapers and magazines go through your hands in the course of a week. Add in the various hymnbooks and Bible versions you encounter in the average church, and how many more books come your way in your workaday life.

Make a list of the way you use books. Manuals for information. Reference books for holiday accommodation. Quality reading for self-improvement. Light casual reading to put you to sleep or to pass the time on a train journey.

By contrast, compare the Ethiopian in Acts 8: 26-40 with us and with very many other Ethiopians in the world today. He is a man in a desert with one book. Reflect on 'the desert'. The outlook may not be as bleak as it first seems.

First, he could at least read. 2000 years later many Ethiopians still can't and literacy figures for other parts of the developing world are no more encouraging. Yet you will probably never hear about it. If they have an earthquake you will hear about that. If they have a famine you will hear about that. But probably not about literacy needs.

Yet severe drought affects people's minds as well as their bodies, and part of the treatment for drought is to stimulate the mind. Reading is a help. And the problems are more acute in a country with a high literacy rate than in a low one, because in a low one at least most people are unable to read, so there is no shame attached to it and alternative methods of conveying information are usually available. On the other hand, the illiterate is at a distinct disadvantage in a country with a high literacy rate.

Second, this man was doubly lucky. He had a book. For the millions in the world who have learned to read there are hundreds of thousands who have nothing to practise on. And reading is like other skills. If you don't use it you soon lose it!

Try to imagine why there is such a shortage. In some cases it is sheer poverty. If you can't afford food, you certainly can't afford books. In others, it is ideology. Some countries do not rate learning and education highly and indeed would prefer their people not to know too much. In others, there are no books because there are no writers, or artists, or publishers, or printers. If the supplies are not there people obviously cannot read.

Third, this Ethiopian had a teacher. The shortage of teachers is one feature of the desert, but the inadequacy of teachers' resources even where they exist is another. Teaching without resources is not impossible, but it does have about it something of the nature of making bricks without straw.

Fourth, in the context of Ascension and the period from Easter to Pentecost, it is perhaps worth reflecting finally that when the teacher had done his job he had to go away and leave the Ethiopian to work it out for himself. Jesus had to go away. Philip had to go away. It is one thing to sense a need, to offer and even to give help. It is an entirely different matter to know how to leave, to trust and to wait. Mary Poppins knew it well!

So instead of looking to the Ascension as something to give inspiration to ourselves (our faith, attitudes, generosity, etc.), try to see it more as an opportunity to give hope and reassurance to the developing nations.

How can we find ways to reassure them that they have much in their favour and enable them to feel that they can get along without us — or at least feel that we are there but they are not dependent on us? Perhaps we have to go away — but how far do we have to go, for how long, and how best can we return?

Misfits

The line between 'the wonder' and 'the misfit' is often a fine one to draw. Begin with the attitude of the locals to Jesus when he returned to Nazareth (Mark 6: 1-6; Matthew 13: 54-8, Luke 4: 16-29). Is the cry in Mark 6: 3 wonder ('fancy us producing this!) or dismissal ('he's nothing but a labourer's lad')? Or is v. 2 wonder (from one group) and v. 3 dismissal (from another)? Or was it something Jesus said or did that changed their attitude? See if you can work out from Luke what it was.

Some characters have the capacity to divide communities just like that.

Identify some in contemporary society. There's probably one in your own family, street, church or club. There are always some in public life and the press will make sure you never miss them: Scargill, Tony Benn, Ian Botham. Make your own list. They have the capacity to draw attention and admiration from some, irritation and rejection from others, and yet nobody can leave them alone.

Look carefully and critically at the havoc they can cause. A child in class, a patient in hospital, a sportsman on the field, a politician at election time.

But then ask how seriously we take them. Do we want to understand or do we want to dismiss? Children may cause havoc because nobody has actually noticed that they are deaf or short-sighted yet they have always been made to sit on the back row. People who spent years in a mental hospital and failed to respond to treatment may have suffered abuse when young which neither they nor their abusers ever wanted to recognize, and society still doesn't.

Choose a few 'Bible misfits' — there are plenty of them — and see what they have to say. The prophet was a misfit as far as Ahab was concerned when he wanted Naboth's vineyard, and though Ahab perhaps could appreciate the point because he had been brought up with people like that, Jezebel who came from a different culture certainly couldn't (I Kings 21). Paul was a misfit, digging things out of the scriptures which many believers had never found before, which they didn't believe were there, and which they didn't want to find if they were!

Jesus was a misfit — with his views on the Sabbath, the foreigner, the prostitute and the tax collector, to name only four. And indeed, he could do nothing very much in Nazareth because they rejected him, and some of them were so incensed that he barely escaped with his life.

When you begin to feel confident with the misfits and your ability to handle them, that is the time to move on to the ones who still give you trouble. Perhaps prominent Christian leaders who question generally recognized doctrine, tradition or morality. Or Christian communities in other races and cultures who reveal a different set of mores, for whom perhaps polygamy or homosexuality are not a problem but alcohol is. People of other faiths or no faith at all? People for whom the community is more important than the individual?

What is it that makes them what they are? What do they say to me? What am I failing to hear?

Try to work out how different the colonialization of South America might have been if it had been imbued with the spirit reflected in *City of Joy* rather than Western imperialism. If only we could have listened to those American Indians (misfits if ever there were any!), might we not have heard something different about true wealth expressed in sanctity, peace, companionship, wisdom, joy and serenity? But that would have taken time, and when time is money time is often what you don't have!

Geoffrey Boycott, bachelor and individualist, often regarded by some as a misfit, not easy for management to handle and not always the most popular member of a team, put a quotation from Thoreau on the flyleaf of his biography: 'If a man does not keep pace with his companions, perhaps it is because he hears a different drummer.'

The Unexpected

If one of the problems for the disciples after the first Easter was learning to recognize Jesus in new forms, their second difficulty, following the Ascension, was learning to acknowledge him in places where they least expected him to be.

Paul's assertion that there is no longer Jew or Greek, slave or free, male or female' (Gal. 3: 28) was to come later and even then was not immediately obvious to all or universally accepted. Some would say it still isn't!

But then those who manage those two hurdles often still have hesitations when they reach the third. This is the realization that even when you find Jesus in unlikely places he isn't necessarily doing what you expect him to be doing. In other words, he isn't necessarily changing the environment as you might wish.

Sometimes he may not be changing it at all — he may simply be living in it. Sometimes he may be changing it but using agents of change which themselves arouse suspicion, or changing beliefs, customs, traditions and practices which many would prefer to leave alone.

Try explaining and understanding that second hurdle in today's world based on a study of Galatians 3: 28. Where are today's 'Jews, Greeks, slaves and females'? Why are we failing to recognize them and what might we do about it?

Then tackle the third hurdle:

— what might he be doing that we would rather not notice?

— what might he be tolerating that we would prefer not to tolerate?

— what agents of change would make us suspicious?

— what changes would we prefer to leave alone?

Things to Do

Choose an aid agency or missionary society and take a close look at travel policy, its intentions and its results, and try to find answers to some pressing questions.

1 How much does it see its work as sending people overseas as workers or missionaries?

— is the emphasis on 'this end and people going' or on the development of local resources and skills?

— does its promotional literature relate stories of 'missionary success and agency contribution' ('You can trust us with your money') or of the creativity and imagination shown by the people to whom it ministers?

2 How much does it concentrate on long- or short-term commitments?

— if short, how useful they are?

— are they just joy-rides for those who go?

— what evidence is there that it learns anything as a result, or that it feeds it back to other people on their return and with what result?

4 What is its policy on sending some of its promotional staff and voluntary workers overseas to see first-hand what is happening? (Try asking the questions under 2 above.)

5 What emphasis is placed on bringing people here?

— who takes the decisions as to who comes and when, and how does that compare with the agency's decision when and where to travel overseas?

— what are the results and who evaluates them?

Once you have done your homework and know exactly whom you want to help, delay no longer.

Begin with three simple, practical steps:

1 Send a love gift as soon as possible and as often as possible, and don't tie it to some particular piece of work.

2 Secure five minutes in your church or other group to talk about what you learn through your gift and make it a basis for prayer and understanding.

3 Try occasionally to focus attention on one aspect of your charity's operations in a church or parish meeting, and if possible try to secure some wider commitment on a one-off basis. (Churches and others are always wary of being dragged into something which is going to go on for ever and possibly exclude other good work which comes along later.)

Local People Know Best?

After working in Bangladesh for 25 years a missionary was told that a sound and extensive literacy proposal on which he had worked for months would not be recommended. It was 'not appropriate to the needs of Bangladesh'. The person making the judgment was a young representative of a large European aid agency who had spent three weeks in the country!

On another occasion a different European aid agency kept an applicant waiting eighteen months (due to reorganization!) for a reply to a request they had marked as 'urgent'. The reply when it came was a series of questions which, with one exception, had been answered in the original proposal, and went on to lay down conditions which the workers in Bangladesh would have had to reject on the basis of their experience and local knowledge. 'The attitude was patronizing and little short of insulting', he added.

Food for Thought — Food for Prayer

THEOLOGICAL EDUCATION

Remember

— a theological college (in Indonesia or Argentina) which is small, where resources are few and the only books they have are a motley collection of those which have been left behind by departing missionaries.

— another where the main theological institution enjoys the full benefits of foreign funds from earlier times, the fruit of missionaries and colonialism, but where the resources for local ministers to train are nil, and a few faculty therefore give their services to establish a new institution.

— extension courses, especially the Education by Extension for Development Action programme (EEDA), based at the Pacific Theological College. which includes Bible teaching, church history in Micronesia, worship and preaching, theology and counselling.

— programmes of accreditation, like that of the Association for Theological Education in South-east Asia, which

— sets standards of attainment and excellence and then encourages colleges to achieve them

— produces literature reflecting local theology and circumstances (contextual theology)

— maintains a pastoral ministry of regular contact and visitation to institutions, faculty and students.

For Confession

Our failure really to listen to the local people, to know what they want, and to appreciate what they can contribute.

For Thanksgiving

Give thanks

— for small operations and groups of people where a few are addressing a particular problem or need

— for the enquiring mind which yesterday gave us 'talking drums' and (more recently) simple benefits for the rural world like hand-wound radios and cassette recorders.

For Others

For Christian lay workers in the islands of the Pacific which are very much colonies of the United States with American-style supermarkets and kitchens and where a kettle will be boiled over a small wood fire side by side with the latest television set.

For those with no voice

For those with a voice — but no strength to use it

For those with strength to speak — but nobody listens

For those who are heard — but misunderstood, misinterpreted or misrepresented

For those who are positively betrayed.

For Ourselves

That we may pray with understanding.

Category

Novels, Poetry and Short Stories reflecting local history, customs or traditions

Remember

Poets, novelists and dramatists broadcasters and historians

Focus On

something from this broad spectrum which enables you to know who you are where you have come from and where you belong, or which has had an effect on your life and faith, and give thanks for the medium (print, air or theatre) which made it possible

---

PRAYER WITH UNDERSTANDING

A missionary complained bitterly because when she was home she went to speak at a school and the head introduced her as coming from India 'where the sun was always shining and it was baking hot'.

So she began by explaining that she came from 8000 feet up in the Himalayas, where it was never hot, where it was frequently very cold and where for many weeks of the year every time you took your clothes out of the wardrobe they were milldew.

That head may have liked to think that he cared about the missionary, but he had never really prayed for her, because he had never tried to understand.

Pray for Accountants

who have to struggle with problems of inflation and cash flow
especially at certain times of the year

PENTECOST
A Time to Wonder

Theme

Everyone was amazed and unable to explain it; they asked one another what it all meant.

Acts 2: 12 (JB)

At Easter the impossible happened to Jesus. At Ascension the disciples began to realize it could happen to them. Pentecost was the first sign that it was.

But as always it wasn't quite what they were expecting nor the way they were expecting it. Their dead were not all coming to life again and any idea of life beyond the grave was still in its infancy.

But something else was happening. Another of God's surprises — to add to the slaves in Egypt and the return from exile! And since they couldn't understand it or explain it they had to be content to wonder at it:

— to wonder that such a diverse group of people had anything in common

— to wonder that in their diversity they could even begin to understand and relate to one another.

It was like a return to Eden! 'Or Babel', sneers the cynic in an attempt to dismiss them. But the similarities with Babel can be creative. That was the last moment, in prehistory, when the whole earth shared one language (Gen 11: 1-9). Today's reader knows that there is all the difference in the world between Babel and Pentecost. Babel was an attempt to achieve a sense of unity borne of self-interest and personal aggrandisement. Pentecost was an attempt to achieve a sense of unity in the name of one who lived, suffered and died for others, *based on a common purpose*. That could never die. That, God established.

So it is better to wonder at what God *is doing* than to worry about what he *did* or how he did it or to try to recreate somewhere else our own understanding of it. And for those with a capacity to wonder there is much in the developing world for them to wonder about.

key word	ruach (Old Testament) means 'breath' and may relate to creation, inspiration, a gift, leadership or judgement. It is 'breath of life', the way God acts in history, the one who empowers the people of God and inspires them for the fulfilment of their mission. pneuma (New Testament) is the fulfilment of the sacred work of Christ among his disciples, the source of the new life within the church and witness to Christ in her mission. At Pentecost pneuma is 'the living energy of a personal God', no longer Jewish-centred but increasingly world-embracing.
πνευμα **Spirit** *ruach* (Hebrew)	

Whose Resources?

In some circles the idea of churches and aid agencies in the West making grants, in money or in kind, in response to requests from Third World churches and agencies, has become increasingly unacceptable. The issues have been around for some twenty years, and ten years ago the World Council of Churches recognized that the time had come for action.

So in 1987, 250 delegates from all over the world held a week's conference at El Escorial and committed themselves 'to a fundamentally new value system', beginning with 'the marginalized taking the centre of all decisions and actions as equal partners' and ending with the promotion and strengthening of 'ecumenical sharing at all levels'.

It is not our purpose to ask whether it worked but to clarify what it was about.

Feelings

Some Third World leaders more than others were embarrassed by having to beg. Some officials in the West and the North were embarrassed to be regarded as 'money-bags'. Most Third World leaders were pleased to receive visitors from overseas and showed no lack of hospitality, but many resented the fact that their work was often subjected to what they regarded as unreasonable scrutiny. They wondered if the same standards of business efficiency were applied to the donating organization back home, and whether some of the business might not have been handled by inviting them to London, or wherever. Some agencies in fact did this, but again Third World visitors couldn't help but notice that their excursions to the West too often coincided with some promotion or fund-raising campaign and naturally felt as if they were being invited 'to sing for their supper'.

Power

Western agencies could always decide to send someone to Delhi or Nairobi. They could also decide to bring someone from Delhi or Nairobi. Officials in Delhi and Nairobi knew their place. Delhi and Nairobi may have a better understanding of what was needed and how to provide it than anyone in London could possibly have but the power to handle it was not theirs. They had no money. To achieve it they had 'to persuade' someone in London that it was a worthwhile need, that their 'solution' was the right one, and that all they needed were the resources.

But then London may not be easily persuaded or may have other 'solutions', and certainly had a different agenda. One agricultural project which was creating landlessness and increasing the gap between rich and poor in Asia was actually kept running for three more years at the insistence of one donor lest their income dropped and they lost confidence among their supporters.

History and Ownership

Until the Second World War most Christian enterprises in the Third World were 'owned' by a Western church or one of their missionary societies. As churches and missionary societies gradually withdrew there was a tendency to make block grants about which no questions were asked followed by further supplementary grants which had to be justified.

Aid agencies worked rather differently. Their funds were raised on a different basis from the missionary societies, often from a different clientèle (the general public as well as the churches), were related to specific areas of need, and in many cases were tied in with government grants. And whereas with the churches proclamation of the gospel had been central and grants secondary, for the aid agencies grants, along with cash and accountability, became dominant. Furthermore, in the interests of efficiency, groups of agencies began to work together. Therefore they had to account not only to their funders but also to one another.

In a strange way aid agencies probably never presumed to 'own' overseas work as the churches and missionary societies had done, yet in a way they assumed more control. So we had the strange situation of the churches withdrawing to give precedence to the local people, only to find the vacuum being filled by the aid agencies.

Third and First World

Ecumenical resource sharing was naturally more popular in the Third World than in the First. They had everything to gain. The First had everything to lose.

Unfortunately perhaps, the debate raised false hopes, and though Western church and aid agencies have made some adjustments there is little evidence that the more far-reaching effects have ever been taken on board.

Apart from the fact that having the discussions at all served to emphasize the very patronizing nature of the aid business which they were designed to amend, three other issues came to the fore.

1   Resource sharing is two-way. 'Reverse flow' is the jargon. We don't give so that they can receive. We learn to share and recognize that Third World churches have a lot to offer in terms of spirituality, theology, ethics and values from which we can benefit.

The sentiments are fine until you apply them, when you discover that we in the West find it hard to receive, that in too many cases the West has little or no interest in what 'they' have to offer (the discovery of which is even more hurtful), and that even among the most spiritual

people hard cash for their own survival is too often more richly treasured than ideas, experiences and theology, nurtured in the Third World but which in the West can be very disturbing.

2   Ownership of resources. The accountability argument rests on the fact that charitable agencies feel they have to be accountable to their donors for the way they spend their money. In some cases this is accepted.

One African agency thought it was perfectly reasonable because, as they saw it, they were 'looking after the donors' money and interests'. That it can be said at all without anger of feeling, in the context of resource sharing, ought of itself to set alarm bells ringing.

Not all recipients would have been so urbane, as comments from India would indicate. Some would certainly want to question whether such resources as the West held had been acquired legally and morally. Others would want to ask whether those with funds, or the ability to raise funds, also have *ipso facto* the right to be the stewards of them and to dispose of them only according to their own wisdom and interests.

3   Ecumenical sharing. Perhaps the most disturbing thing to come to light in the debate was the inability of many churches and missionary societies in the West to share with each other. Each had their own bit of the globe, their own 'expertise', their own contacts. They treasured them, felt a responsibility for them, and would argue that without direct grant-making they might lose touch with them altogether. Co-operation was possible — just — but any open commitment to any wider body was suspect. Introduce the aid agencies and the picture was even more complicated.

Empires certainly don't self-destruct! But is it wrong at least to expect Christian ones to self-sacrifice?

CHILDREN ON THE STREET

Using Writing and Creating Literature — to change attitudes

In the Philippines you must distinguish children OFF the street and children ON the street.

Children OFF the street tend to be runaways and orphans, very mobile, not normally organized as gangs, earning money by collecting garbage, picking up plastic cups and selling them back for re-cycling, always liable to be exploited by the syndicates and even by the police, because sometimes it is easier to pull in these children than it is to go after the real culprits.

Children ON the street have homes and families to go to, and probably spend half their day in school and half working. These are the real street vendors.

Some sell plastic bags. Armed with one peso they buy a batch first thing in a morning, knowing from experience where they can get the best deal. They sell at a small profit and go back for more. By the end of the day some will have earned enough to buy a kilo of rice for a family for two meals, and possibly even enough to buy two pieces of fish.

Others are cigarette vendors, sometimes known as 'jump-boys', jumping on the 'Jeepneys' (local buses), offering a cigarette and a light and then jumping off again. Some are newsboys. Some sell lottery tickets, accumulating cash by buying astutely and exploiting the twin emotions of typical Filipino adults who, being fatalistic, always hope the next one will be the winner, yet who also have a deep sense of charity and can therefore console themselves with the thought that even if they don't win they may help somebody.

Such street vending activities are not without risk, and this was what drew the attention of some socially-caring staff members of the Asia Social Institute. The problem was how to handle it. Story books for children seemed to be the answer! But who could write in a style and language those children would ever read? Did they read story books anyway? And since very often a whole family was living off their earnings, how could you even thinking of taking them off the streets?

So for a whole year they simply befriended the children, observed their behaviour and tried to gain their confidence. To gain the parents' confidence the parish priest introduced them as evidence of the honesty of the research they were doing.

They invited children to a meeting at head-quarters. They discovered how, during their working hours, the street was a work place, a meeting place, a dining room, a toilet and almost everything else. They encouraged them to produce drawings which reflected their lives.

From this confidence, and from the children's drawings and ideas, grew a series of four books, two for the 6-9 year olds and two for the 9-12 year olds, designed not only to help the children ON the street to understand that there is an alternative way of life, but also to change the attitudes of their parents and other children, as well as teachers and adults in the churches: to explain that the poor are not necessarily lazy or dishonest, and that they do have a value and contribute to the life of the family.

PAUL COUTURIER

The Man whose Concern for Refugees led him to see the Call for Christian Unity as the Essence of Oikumene

There are two reasons for celebrating Christian unity around Pentecost rather than during the Octave of Prayer for Christian Unity in January.

One is that the January emphasis was started by two Anglicans in 1908 with the express purpose of leading the Anglican Church back to Rome. The other is that when it is associated with Pentecost it takes us beyond the unity of Christians to the unity of all humanity in Christ. And one man who helps us to achieve that broader reference is the French Roman Catholic, the Abbé Paul Couturier.

Born in 1881, Couturier spent most of his life in relative obscurity in Lyons. Not being equipped for the parish he spent most of his time as a professor, but it was said that his students did not even 'nibble' at his lessons, being influenced more by the sanctity which radiated from him and by the profound words which expressed the closeness of his relationship with God.

Realizing the inadequacy of a unity movement which thought only in terms of 'returning to the fold', Couturier preached that all of us must be converted to Christ.

With that conviction three main influences brought him from professorial obscurity to the heart of the movement for Christian unity, and all of them point to emphases which are now largely lost or overlooked.

1   In the region where Couturier lived there were about 10,000 Russian refugees, and having acknowledged the primacy of charity in all his work Couturier welcomed these exiled Christian brethren with open arms, and tried to listen to them and enter into their situation. Through refugees he learned to love the saints of the Russian Church and entered into correspondence with leaders of the Orthodox community, but his response also demonstrates the importance of hearing the call to unity in a secular situation and developing it on a broader platform than simply the ecclesiastical.

2   Twelve years later, he paid a visit to the Benedictines at Amay, Belgium. This community had been founded by the Pope a few years earlier and was concerned to bring about a reconciliation between divided Christendom and a new understanding between the church of the East and the church of the West.

3   At Amay he met Cardinal Mercier, who had already established contacts with Anglican theologians and who was himself set on the task of establishing Christian unity. From him he learned what was happening towards unity and also the value of personal friendships.

This latter point he turned to practical account when he got back to Lyon by arranging opportunities for RC and Protestant theologians to meet and talk. Then, knowing that talking was not enough, he put the emphasis on prayer and believed that problems would be seen in a new light once they were discussed in a spirit of prayer and friendship.

He was described on one occasion as 'an apparition of love' and at his funeral in 1953 as 'the apostle and the undaunted worker for the unity of all Christians'. [7.1]

AMBON TO KAMAL

Indonesian ministers learn their craft in the rural areas

Ambon, one of the 13,677 islands of Indonesia, boasts one state and three Private universities (one Presbyterian, one Roman Catholic, one Muslim). The Presbyterian one began as a theological school in 1965 and acquired university status in 1985 when three other faculties were added. Total enrolment is just over two thousand, with a third studying theology. Both staff and students include Muslims.

The school, with a strong social concern, has created a social rural laboratory at Kamal, on the neighbouring island of Seram, to provide training not only for students but also for pastors, women and young people.

Kamal is one hour by ferry and another by car from Ambon, and very different, but in a country which is 85% rural, ministers who have begun life in an urban area need to know what it is like to live in a village.

Students go for three months. Before moving out into the remoter parts of the island they spend one month in conditions virtually identical to those of the rural people whom they will serve. They live in two wooden huts, one for men, one for women. Two wooden benches run the length of the hut and they have about two feet of space each. Cooking is in the open. Washing dries in the warm sun.

Kamal is more than student training. It is a 'think tank' for the Ambon churches to discover how to develop Christian congregations in a modern world, how to give enrichment to theological studies, how to relate students in the other faculties to theology, and how church leaders can take advantage of interdisciplinary studies.

Kamal is also a place to observe the impact of social change in a situation where nothing has changed for hundreds of years. It is a study of what happens when people are dispossessed of their land and migrants move in, when new industries arrive and old ones die, and how people of widely diverse background can actually begin to become one: to learn to communicate with each other and to discover common interests. Students are encouraged to ask questions about change and so strengthen their theological understanding of life.

Most of the migrants are from Java, part of a government scheme to reduce the population in Java and to give people more space by moving them out and giving them two acres of land each. The Roman Catholic Church has also bought land, put up a building and invited members in Java to come and develop it, and one result is that on an island where rice was never grown paddy fields are springing up everywhere.

Not all the changes are good, however, and this is one reason for a Christian social laboratory on the spot. Factories and industry, just up the road from the laboratory, are beginning to produce plywood (one of Indonesia's major exports), and as one man put it, 'One plywood factory arrives and the world moves several degrees and begins to turn on a different axis.'

First, it took their land. Then their jobs. Then it offered other jobs for which the locals were not qualified, so in came the migrant workers. Its effluents poisoned the sea, their main source of fish and food, and people who have never had to work hard because the land and the sea were so productive suddenly need lots of help to live with shortage, competition and pollution.

Assessing the impact of such changes on the community and helping the community to cope with it is seen as an important part of theological training. Kamal provides three opportunities:

1 To see the change taking place in embryo.

2 To help theological students to relate theology to the world they are living in.

3 To learn what it means to live and work in a rural situation, to enter into the rural mind, and to see what happens in a time of change or crisis. 'Crisis is a good time for intervention', said one.

Pastors as Agents of Change

A Christian Education Centre, working among the more conservative churches and ministers in Quito, Ecuador, recently set about change by introducing ministers to study which brought together Bible and World, and related them especially to the problems of Ecuador.

Church members were encouraged to engage in theological study which enabled them to move and work effectively beyond the frontiers of the church; to get out of the ivory tower, to stop seeing themselves as a separate body and judging the rest of the world as 'sinners'.

Ministers, in turn, were encouraged to become 'liberated people' and then 'agents of change'. Their course of study covered their own family, the Bible, the church and the community. And since none of them read or wrote very much the course concentrated less on literature and more on cassettes and personal contact.

DRUGS AND BOOKS

The *Observer* recently reported that the international pharmaceuticals industry is up in arms about moves to stem the flood of inappropriate drug donations to the Third World.

Hundreds of millions of dollars-worth of drugs are donated each year in the guise of philanthropy by companies seeking cheap waste disposal, enlarged markets and generous tax write-offs.

The World Health Organization says such 'gifts' can hamper international relief operations, imperil national health strategies, and saddle Third World countries with mountains of Western toxic waste needing disposal.

Although part of the problem is small, well-meaning charities collecting cast-off drugs from pharmacies and dispensaries, the bigger culprits are the manufacturers, who give huge consignments to charities for 'placing' overseas.

Similar comments could be made about books, particularly where losses are written off by bulk consignments to Third World countries and then entered in the accounts as gifts to charities. [7.2]

NO MULTIPLE THROWOUTS, PLEASE!

ABC lectures at the XYZ Theological College in (wherever you want) and says they are desperately in need of Christian books in English for use by staff and students. 'We particularly need Bible commentaries, dictionaries, reference works and books of all kinds on theology, pastoral care and mission.'

So reads a notice in the religious press, nearly always in the same form. Sometimes it adds that Professor ABC is visiting this country and can arrange to take them back.

It is a sign of the desperation that leads a man to lug heavy books half way around the world. It touches everybody who cares about books or education and has even only an inkling of what a Third World college library can be like. No wonder he gets a response. **But how much does it really help?**

THE POWER OF ADDICTION

In a way it is very hard for me not to accept help for my organization because there is so much need to eliminate poverty, illiteracy, ignorance and disease, coupled with social injustice and political bigotry.

We do need help and we must get out of this wretched situation of helplessness and live as other human beings live in this world.

I also know that any help that comes free of cost has the power of addiction.

Once we settle down in this position we may never be able to shake this addiction off.

This thought haunts many of us.

Indian Christian Leader

In most cases, probably about as much as raiding your larder to send a few packets of powdered soup, jelly or blancmange plus a few tins of baked beans, meat and fish to a relatively unknown address in a time of famine in Ethiopia.

It certainly helps the senders. They feel as if they have done something even if not much. It helps the recipients, in that something is better than nothing, though whether the food is the sort they want, whether it is the sort they ought to have, whether it will generally help or hinder their health, whether they know how to cook it and, of course, whether they even have a tin-opener and the capacity to read the label, are questions too many donors would rather not ask. But what is the alternative?

In the case of food (though not yet sadly in the case of clothes and imperishables) most of us have learned to work through one of the main aid agencies, to ensure that gifts are suitable and appropriate, are what the recipients really need and are likely to get to the right place and have a reasonable chance of being wisely used. We have also learned that providing them with the skills and resources to grow the crops they like and need is better than either.

As with hunger so with books. Except for technical, standard theological reference books the real answer to countless heart-rending appeals from Third World churches and colleges is not multiple throwouts but a carefully planned policy. Some books are desperately needed. Others (often the ones people are most keen to throw out) are not. Some places need lots. Others are starving.

But most important of all is not books but support (usually money) to enable them to produce their own titles reflecting their own culture, and sadly too much indiscriminate collection and shipping of books actually undermines rather than helps.

CONTINUED EXPLOITATION

After the Cold War — what?

Visiting Russia shortly after the end of the Cold War was a painful experience for anyone who cared for the Russian people and was anxious that the mistakes of the empire and colonialisation were not to begin all over again.

David Hearst, Moscow correspondent for *The Guardian*, summed up the danger when he described three fellow-passengers on a BA flight to Moscow.

The Belgian pointed down to the hangar — they had bought it! The German was buying up something else. The third man called himself 'a missionary from the Lord'. 'They were missionaries for no one but themselves,' said Hearst.

The West certainly moved in — and quickly. McDonalds, Wimpys and Coca Cola appeared overnight, though sometimes in two distinct halves, one on the left for the roubles and the other on the right for foreign currency.

The more fundamentalist churches, and not a few of the mainstream ones as well, moved in with undignified haste to save the lost, promote the Bible and sell their books.

And the Russians bought it because they too believed it was all going to work. Nationalism would take over from Communism. Western democracy, pop songs, goodies in the shops — who could blame them for dreaming of a white Christmas! The fault was not in those who 'bought' so much as those who 'deceived to sell'.

Today the scene is somewhat different. The free market may have arrived, says Hearst, but the belief that the West would help Russia has gone. Advocates of the trickle-down theory should ask themselves how much of this newly-created wealth has trickled down to within fifty miles of the major cities, and to whom. 'The missionaries have long since flown home,' he writes. 'The quick bucks have been made, and what Russian industry needs is investors, not asset-strippers.'

Similarly with the churches. How much of all the money and effort expended in Eastern Europe has brought real and lasting benefit to the ordinary members and small rural churches of the East, and how much has succeeded in simply extending the aid empires of the churches of the West? [7.3]

TELETHON

In 1988, Telethon welcomed Nicholas Scott, who handed over to £1 million which his government department had withheld from the unemployed.

CIN devotes £450,000 a year to the Family Welfare Association for which social workers can apply on behalf of children with emergency needs.

The FWA certainly requires that money but only because the Government has withdrawn Single Payment Grants which used to give poor families statutory access to help for emergencies. [7.4]

POWER AND BALANCE
WALLS OR NO WALLS

'Let us imagine anywhere on the planet a country which has mile-high walls instead of conventional boundaries. After a period of, say, a thousand years, the walls crumble, and for the first time curious outsiders can see what sort of a society has evolved within. They will find, of course, a more or less large group on top that holds power — political and economic — over a more or less large group underneath which submits to this power.

But the thousand year history of this fantasy country will show that there has always been a limit beyond which the powerful group could not go without provoking revolt on the part of the underlings: without automatically insuring its own overthrow. So if the powerful group have been reasonably benevolent, if disparities in living standards between them and those over whom they hold sway have not been too glaring, we may find that the same class has perpetuated its control for the whole of the thousand years.

If, on the other hand, each powerful group has repressed those beneath them beyond the limits of human endurance, even the most refined police methods the society has been able to devise will not have prevented several upsets from taking place. A sort of physical equilibrium establishes itself between the interests of the dominating and the dominated — the former cannot tread too heavily on the latter without causing serious imbalance in the system and eventually their own downfall and replacement.

Now let us imagine the same country without any walls, and on the contrary with totally permeable frontiers. The dominant class in the country is still repressing those beneath, but sensing their growing restiveness, it looks for allies. It finds them in the dominant groups of other countries with which it can communicate, and who share, on the whole, its principal goals.

If our country's dominant class can do so without really sacrificing its own privileges — which are control over part of the country's wealth and over the productive labour of its own poor — it will seek out the most powerful allies it can find. Usually the latter will be only too glad to oblige. Both groups will get something out of the deal. But the previous natural balance between repression and revolt within the country will have been destroyed in the process.' [7.5]

LES MISÉRABLES

'People reduced to the extremity of need are also driven to the utmost limits of their resources, and woe to any defenceless person who comes in their way. Work and wages, food and warmth, courage and goodwill — all is lost to them. The daylight dwindles into shadow and darkness enters their hearts; and within this darkness man seizes upon the weakness of woman and child and forces them into ignominy.

No horror is then excluded. Desperation is bounded only by the flimsiest of walls, all giving access to vice and crime . . . they appear utterly depraved, corrupt, vile and odious; but it is rare for those who have sunk so low not to be degraded in the process, and there comes a point, moreover, where the unfortunate and infamous are grouped together, merged in a single fateful world. They are Les Misérables — the outcasts, the underdogs.'

Victor Hugo

CHOOSING A CHARITY
Some Questions to Ask

Choice is a privilege. It is also a responsibility. Parents who never had a choice which school they sent their children to are usually pleased to be told that there are several options — until they realize that making a decision requires a lot of hard work, careful questioning and wise evaluation. League tables may not be all that they seem! Choosing a bank, an insurance company, a pension or (for that matter) even a church is no easier.

So how do you choose a charity? If you know precisely who or what you want to help it may not be too difficult. The choice may be very small. But suppose you want to make a contribution to the broad problems of the developing world or to some international disaster.

Most of the big aid agencies are likely to be involved and their natural links with government and media will afford them an air of respectability. But how do you know which to give your money to?

There is no easy answer but, like those parents, if you really want to exercise your choice there is some hard work you can do.

1 Study their accounts. How much income have they and how much do they distribute? From that you ought to be able to assess their overheads or promotion costs. But then look more carefully. If they report surprisingly low promotion costs, find out what those costs cover. Overheads and administration costs may be set out somewhere else. Some promotion costs may be dressed up to look like education, some administration costs may be described as research and development, and some staff salaries may be allocated to an overseas project or two.

None of this need suggest anything wrong but it may mean that the immediate picture is not as it appears and could be misleading when compared with other charities of the same kind.

Once you have established the overall salaries bill, you can ask other questions. Many people, for example, would be suspicious of a charity paying high wages, and perhaps they should be. But others, with equal justification, would be just as suspicious of one which paid low — they may be developing a good reputation for helping the poor in one place while actually taking advantage of the poor on their own staff, or they may be employing incompetent staff and, if they are, the whole organization may be suffering from waste and inefficiency.

2 Study their size. There are two extreme arguments here. One says the big charity is better because there is an economy of scale, more experience, efficiency etc. The other says the small charity is better because the overheads are lower (not necessarily true) and the staff are more personally and individually committed.

Both have some truth on their side. Perhaps in the end it is a personal matter. Just as some people like big families and others small, or some like working for large combines whereas others prefer a small firm, so we choose our charities according to personal preference. But even so, it is at least worth taking a look at size in relation to the job to be done, or the benefits and liabilities of competition in relation to the number of other charities doing the same work.

3 Study their mode of operation. One view is that charities in the developing world need to have good people on the ground in order to plan, organize or supervise the projects. Another is

that Westerners on the ground are not the most effective way of helping because they crush local initiative and prevent the indigenous growth which enables projects to continue successfully once the aid workers have withdrawn.

Try to find out whether they send equipment or money. Some agencies believe money to be a hazard and boast that they only send equipment. If so, check whether they are sending new equipment or old equipment.

If it is second-hand (or, worse still, somebody's 'cast-offs') be doubly cautious. Too often old equipment is handed over to people with no expertise in using it and no training facilities, and breaks down soon after it arrives, often where there is no servicing agent or (if there is) there are no spare parts for that particular model.

If it is new, check that the people receiving it have been adequately trained to handle it and that there are servicing agents on hand.

Ask where it will be purchased. Sometimes aid agencies make a grant of money for equipment provided it is purchased in their own country regardless of whether the people on the receiving end think that country is supplying the best product for their purposes. Government agencies are the worst offenders in this regard because it is a way of using their overseas aid budget in order to support their own industry.

Ask who chose it. Was it the people giving it or the people receiving it? Who then, in your judgment, knew best what was most appropriate for that local situation, and who is likely to be more satisfied if it succeeds and more disappointed, if not angry, if it fails?

If, on the other hand, an agency sends only money, other questions may need to be addressed, like who decides how much the gift should be. Is it the local people saying what their carefully worked out plans and estimates require or is it the agency saying what they are willing to give? How much discussion and negotiation takes place, and how much freedom has the recipient in spending it? Is it a lump sum for a broad project? Or a detailed and itemized list which the local people have to live with even if it is not quite what they think they want or circumstances change and make some of it futile as they go along?

What control is there over either? Is there a balance between freedom and control, and if there is, how is it arrived at?

4 Study their claims to be 'Christian'. At best, if a charity claims to be Christian you can know that it accepts a basic set of beliefs and ethical principles and if you are disturbed by reports or ever have reason to question what is going on you have a common set of principles to which you can turn. At worst, you can have recourse to a kind of 'Christian blackmail', such as 'can you really justify that kind of behaviour in a Christian organization?'

But do not assume that because an agency has 'Christian' in its title there are no further questions to ask. You may want to ask what it means. Does it mean their income comes only from Christians or do they not mind where it comes from? Does it mean their aid is restricted to Christians only or do they offer help to everybody? If it is restricted to Christians, is it all who claim to be Christian or only those brands of 'Christian' that the charity approves of? And does 'Christians only' mean they only support 'religious' activities, such as Bibles, church buildings and Christian education, or do they support Christian programmes in their wholeness, such as food, health and literacy? If they do, what then is their motivation for helping others? Is it truly open-ended or is it intended as a starting point for proselytization?

After that, all the other questions apply just as much to a Christian organization as to any other.

THE CUTTING EDGE

The Association for Theological Education in South East Asia (ATESEA) is one of fifty similar associations around the world. Though they vary considerably in size and the detail of their work their overall objective is the same.

ATESEA is one of the more highly organized. Its aim is to set standards, monitor and generally to raise the level of theological education. An important feature of their work is a visit to every accredited theological school once every three to five years, plus visits to schools who are seeking accreditation, in order to report to their executive committee, which decides whether the particular degree or diploma comes up to the required standard. If not, the Association has a series of notations to help an institution to see what steps it has to take to achieve it.

Notations may relate to admission standards, curriculum and field education, community life and spiritual formation, finance, library, staff-student ratio, staff qualifications, staff research and development, relationships with church and other academic institutions, student participation in decision-making, the number of women involved at all levels, not to mention buildings, grounds and equipment.

ATESEA keeps in close touch with theological institutions in Indonesia, Burma, Hong Kong, the Philippines, Taiwan, Malaysia, Pakistan, Singapore, Sri Lanka, Thailand, Vietnam, Australia and New Zealand. It produces the *Asia Journal of Theology* and relates closely to the South East Asia Graduate School of Theology, which besides having Master's and Doctoral programmes engages also in programmes of research and development. It receives a certain amount of funding which it allocates among the schools and runs its own modest publishing programme, mainly contextual theology.

THE CHANGING FACE

The **Pacific Regional Seminary,** Fiji, is a Roman Catholic institution founded in 1972 with 18 students. Today there are over 100. It serves 14 dioceses, all tiny clusters of islands separated by vast distances.

Its commitment is to train priests in the context of the cultural, social, spiritual and theological needs of the Catholic Church throughout Micronesia, Polynesia and Melanesia where Catholics represent 10%-15% of the local population, most of the others being Christians of other traditions.

After four years of academic studies students spend one year in pastoral practice in their home diocese before returning to the seminary for a final two years. Most students then undertake further work in their local dioceses before being called to ordination. The main language of the seminary is English and they have a library of 15,000 titles.

The Pacific Theological College, Fiji, is a parallel Protestant institution where a team of 10 international teachers cater for 50 or 60 students and the library is strong in biblical studies.

An Education by Extension for Development Action programme (EEDA) is a correspondence course with three weeks residential training once a year, mainly for the islands of Micronesia where almost none of the pastors has had any theological training.

Holding Hands

The Week of Prayer for Christian Unity is variously celebrated in January, in May or whenever, but Pentecost and Christian unity are inseparable. The High Priestly Prayer of John 17 has long been the focus (especially vv. 20-21), but for too long those words have been interpreted in terms of church unity rather than Christian unity, as our earlier reference to Paul Couturier testifies.

When you look closely at John 17, three things become clear. One, it is a prayer for the believers — they are the ones Jesus is concerned about. Two, he wants believers to demonstrate the unity he enjoys with the Father. Three, why? So that the world might believe.

Concentrate on the phrase, 'that they may be one even as we are one', and explore the unity between Father and Son. This is no normal relationship and there are many ways of appreciating it, but for our purposes explore it in terms of a generous father and an obedient son in a divided world, because failure here could be the cause of some of much disunity.

Spend time thinking of ways in which believers of all persuasions and theological outlooks have difficulty with the generosity of God.

— moral generosity. Believers who give themselves to single parents, alcoholics, homosexuals and lesbians, or other 'social outcasts' often find the generosity of God more accessible than the generosity of their fellow believers who find it hard to understand their commitment or who are deeply worried by it.

— doctrinal generosity. Long before *Honest to God* and ever since, any doctrinal or theological deviation has been a worry to some.

What does it mean to call an unknown people, slaves in Egypt, and entrust them on an open ticket with the Ten Commandments? Or a man of doubtful reputation like David to become the father of a nation? Or a tax collector, a Peter or a Judas, or even a carpenter's son? All very dodgy! Whatever will people think? Start down that road and who knows where you will finish up!

But then are we any better with an obedient son? It is a convenient argument that it is our obedience to the son which prevents us from accepting a too-generous father, but is it really obedience to the son or is it obedience to something in ourselves?

The main thrust of this prayer, for example, is that the disciples would not be taken out of the world, yet is it not often the case that those whose attitudes are least generous, and whose claims to obedience are loudest, are the ones who want to keep themselves and their friends unspotted from the world?

Examine the temptations to turn any local church into a cosy club. Are any young people welcome at the youth activities or only those who . . . ? If the church has a home for the elderly is it for any elderly or only for those who . . . ? And how often in public worship does the mention of individuals to make them feel that 'they belong' have the effect of making others, especially visitors and newcomers, feel that they don't?

Jesus's prayer is that his disciples will be faithful in the world, not taken out of it. That is an expression of the unity between generosity and obedience. It is the prayer of a world-accepting saviour, not afraid to get his hands dirty.

How many of us can follow him? How far, and for how long? Hand-washing is not confined to Pilate. Think of some examples, like preachers who feel they have to make disclaimers when they recommend books lest what they recommend turns out to be unacceptable or others who say they hate the sin but love the sinner.

Think hard about the self-isolating and patronizing ways in which many church programmes are promoted. We talk about being 'in solidarity with the poor' as if to emphasize that none of us is poor. Or about 'strengthening the arm of the poor', as if our arm was unquestionably stronger. Or about what the churches might do 'for the unemployed' as though nobody in the church was unemployed. And on one occasion when the churches had a 'Hands Across the Nation for Unemployment' hand-holding exercise, which sounded impeccable, they had to spoil it by saying it was not a political act, when everybody knows that unemployment is a political issue and can only be solved by politics. No dirt on our hands — in the name of one who had blood on his side!

How many more phrases can you think of which reveal our hand-washing and superiority? Church unity is domestic. Christian unity is Pentecostal. It relates to the whole created order.

Soon after Jesus uttered this prayer it became clear that it would only be answered in suffering — his suffering! Is that what we mean by holding hands? Hanging on to a generous God? Joining forces with an obedient son? Holding hands even in the darkness of its pain . . . until the world believes? It could take a very long time!

Joel's Vision

Whilst Western churches celebrate Pentecost in terms of Joel's prophecy (about pouring out the Spirit 'on all flesh', young men 'seeing visions', old men 'dreaming dreams'), and recognize the importance of such diverse nations sitting down together and learning a new way of relating to each other (Joel 3: 28 and Acts 2: 1-11), most of them will then readily revert to a policy of preserving what they have inherited rather than risk losing it for the possibility of a new discovery, and any suggestion of engaging in worship or sharing churches with people who hold another faith will still cause nightmares.

So forget for the moment the traditional interpretations about the coming of the Spirit. Take a look instead at those in whom he works.

Identify today's Parthians, Medes, Elamites, etc.

— people who literally speak a different language

— people who belong to a different culture or social stratum, or who accept a different set of mores

— people who are committed to a different faith, or no faith at all

— people who hitherto had had little or no contact with each other

— the people who sneer (Acts 2: 13).

Imagine what happens when these groups actually meet, or are invited to sit together around the same table (or altar).

— what are their first reactions?

— what *real* problems do they face?

— what *imaginary* problems do they create?

— what are their feelings towards each other?

— to what extent do they actually want to hear and to understand?

Try in one or two sentences to summarize what Peter brings to the situation by his sermon (Acts 2: 16-36.) Work out what it means in today's world.

Alternatively, explore the idea of Pentecost as a summons to a common purpose:

— a worldwide humanitarianism such as we find hinted at in Deuteronomy and developed further in Luke's Gospel

— a recognition that not self-aggrandizement but self-effacement and suffering to the point of death are the gateway to life.

Where these features are to be found then a new spirit of unity and understanding, leading to a new sense of unity and belonging, will be born, but what is needed initially from us?

SOME INDIANS SPEAK OUT

On Ownership

Donors collect money and have a responsibility to use it well. But they also have an interest in staying in business. When Zacchaeus realized he had defrauded he immediately promised restitution fourfold. He didn't say, 'If I give you back what I took what would you do with it?'

On Influence

Donors, even with the best intentions, do try to influence aid programmes. Europeans in particular have many hang-ups, especially guilt, and some of their representatives seem to think they know what is best for everybody. Some of their ideology too is very Western and they are anxious to export this.

On Dependency

Christian churches must find some way of getting out of the dependency which aid programmes create. At one time missionaries used to give clothes and food and that was good, but the trouble was it created emotional satisfaction for the missionaries as well as for the receivers who came to depend on them.

On Communism

In the 1950s Western governments were afraid countries like China and India would go Communist and get out of hand. Hence their desire to keep these countries reasonably under control and so preserve their standard of living in the West. Their ability to continue to live and make their contribution to humanity requires them to give aid. Giving is the only activity that retains leadership and keeps their society alive and if it fails then others may do it and the power of the West could be eclipsed.

Things to Do

POWER SHARING

Power Sharing, like Resource Sharing, is a popular concept in aid and development circles, especially among church, aid and mission agencies, but what are the realities?

How much is it a topic for books and articles, education and conferences, and how much an active policy?

Try asking an agency, through its representative if they pay you a visit, what its policy on power sharing is.

Then, if you want to know how much an aid agency recognizes the people whom it supports, here are ten questions you might pursue, separately and independently, to help you find out:

1 Who determines which countries and which organizations are helped?

2 What committee makes the decisions?

3 Where does it meet?

4 Who appoints the members?

5 Who writes the agenda?

6 Who drafts the papers? And who re-drafts them?

7 Who speaks? And who listens?

8 Who finally decides? And who draws up the terms?

9 Who signs the cheque? And who decides when the money is released?

10 In which country do they live?

Finally, try to make contact with one or two groups whom they support and put the same questions to them. How far is their perception and feeling the same as that of the aid agency?

YOUR FAVOURITE CHARITY

Look critically at one or two charities operating in the field of development, especially your favourite.

Read their literature. Look at their accounts. Ask a few questions:

1 How much is short-term relief and how much long-term planning? Which do you want to support?

2 What emphasis do they place on training local people and developing local industry or activity? One way of getting at this is to ask what would actually continue if they suddenly had to pull out tomorrow.

3 How much is going on the people there and how much on HQ, promotion and advertising, and UK workers overseas?

4 Talk to people with specialist knowledge of the sort of work they are supporting: doctors and nurses if it is health, nutritionists if it is food, publishers and booksellers if it is literature, and people in the emergency services if it is disaster and relief.

Listen to the issues they raise. Try to find out how seriously your charity is aware of the issues and has taken them on board.

5 If one of the West's problems is learning to receive and responding to what the developing countries have to offer, how much of the charity's effort goes into creating that interest and helping Westerners to appreciate its value?

6 How willing is your charity to share what *we* have and *they* need when it may not be what we would like to give, e.g. skills in fund-raising.

Certain Third World communities know there are resources to be tapped in their own country and would love to do so but need help to know where to begin.

Is this something your charity is willing to contemplate?

SOME OTHER REACTIONS

On Resource Sharing

'. . . despite various advances on one front or another, the fundamental situation has not changed. Everyone always speaks well of proposals for more authentic sharing, and everyone keeps acting in much the same way as in the past.'

— *Philip Potter, then General Secretary of the World Council of Churches, speaking at a conference on resource sharing prior to El Escorial, 1987*

On Charity

The enjoyment derived from charity is a haughty and immoral enjoyment. The rich man's enjoyment (lies in) his wealth, his power, and in the comparison of his importance with that of the poor. Charity corrupts giver and taker alike; and, what is more, (charity) does not attain its objects as it only increases poverty.

— *The Devils* (Dostoevsky)

At a British Churches' Conference on Resource Sharing one delegate rose to ask if in future they could have the benefit of a document in good, clear English, the basic document before them having been written in 'ecumenical Esperanto'. It was a fair comment on the document. But consider!

English is a resource we have shared with the world. We can hardly expect it to be in the form it was before when it comes back to us. And if we cannot cope with what happens when we share our language how can we begin to think about sharing anything else?

Food for Thought
— Food for Prayer

INDONESIA

Use the stories from Indonesia and the work of ATESEA as the basis for prayers on the whole world of theological education. Pray for . . .

— colleges trying to balance numbers with the need to maintain standards and a satisfactory staff-student ratio of 15:1.

— faculty struggling to find time and money for travel and research so as to improve their teaching and develop their potential.

— students who need work to pay fees where work is virtually non-existent.

— students suffering loss of community in colleges where living accommodation is nil or partial.

— students with limited library facilities in terms of books, space, light and air-conditioning, or where a limited knowledge of English makes the use of specialist books extremely difficult.

— church leaders and publishers who have difficulty finding writers to produce more books in their own language.

— over-worked faculty with an ability to write but little time to do it.

— librarians struggling with limited budgets and cataloguing facilities.

Category

Christian Magazines,
Journals and Periodicals of all kinds
RE Textbooks, Children's Literature and
Popular Paperbacks

Remember

Popular writers, newsagents
street vendors and teachers

Focus On

one children's story which has lived
with you all your life.
Give thanks for the person who wrote it and
those who enabled its publication

CHILDREN

Give thanks for

— the skills, resourcefulness and achievements of children, especially in the Philippines

— the commitment of those who try to help them, and who appreciate what it is that puts them there in the first place

— teachers with insight and imagination to help children to produce their own books and begin to solve their own problems

— researchers studying consumer patterns and the role of the media, assessing the problems of tribal minorities and raising questions as to how to live in a minority situation

— an appreciation of the variety of ways in which imagination and creativity can use education and literature to such positive ends.

Pray for Production Managers

who have to find suitable printers
and cope with paper shortages and printer delays

POST-PENTECOST
A Time to Celebrate

Theme

Let it be known to you that this salvation of God has been sent to the Gentiles; they will listen.

Acts 28: 28 (NRSV)

As long as we can restrict this incident to the battle between the Jews and the Gentiles we are safe. For Christianity, it was over long ago. But scratch the surface and you soon strike the rock of offence again. For 'Jews' read 'Christians'. For 'Gentiles' read 'the world', 'the unbeliever' or 'people of other faiths'.

Paul's problem was that he had dared to cross swords with the religious establishment whose job it was to protect the *status quo*. He had openly questioned (if not rejected!) the faith of the centuries. He had become the ring-leader of a sect (Acts 24: 5). And if the faithful had had their way they would have killed him. He was saved by the secular authorities of the Roman Empire. Some of the European reformers were not so fortunate. Of all powers and authorities those of the religious establishment can be among the most cruel.

But whilst the faithful were demonstrating their blindness (Isa. 6: 9-10; Mark 4: 12; Acts 26: 7), Gentiles were demonstrating their capacity to see,

and this only aggravated the problem. Hence Paul's final words, '. . . this salvation of God has been sent to the Gentiles; they will listen' (Acts 28: 28).

The faithful are always in danger of prevarication and internecine warfare while the Spirit moves in other places and the world comes to believe. With an uncluttered eye they have a unique clarity of vision. Blind eyes may actually perceive more than people with sight who always know exactly what they are looking at. So, whilst the faithful are blind and deaf, the world comes to believe and the faithful find it hard to come to terms with it.

Problems became more acute in the post-Pauline period. The Jews softened or came to terms with the inevitable. Perhaps Yahweh *was* at work in other places. Perhaps those of The Way could be regarded as part of 'the faithful' as long as they became Jews first. 'No', said the church. 'Christians, yes — Jews, never'. God cannot possibly be tied to one particular religious grouping. Creator of all. Father of all. Redeemer of all.

key word	*oikoumene* originally meant the inhabited world (Luke 2: 1). Since then it has been used variously for the bringing together of all Roman Catholics (in the Ecumenical Councils) and of Christians from many churches worldwide (since Edinburgh 1910), but is now slowly re-establishing its place in relation to the whole inhabited world by its emphasis on social and political action to secure freedom, aid, justice and peace, and to relate the gospel to all spheres of society.
ΟΙΚΟΥΜΕΝη The whole inhabited world	

Some Literacy Questions

Just how important is literacy? 'The very foundation of a modern society,' says one. 'The only way to handle poverty,' says another. 'The key to education, which is the only thing that is going to improve the lot of millions,' says a third. 'Crucial for women,' says a fourth. 'Not so important if you live in a country where most people can read,' says a fifth. 'Of less importance as we move into the electronic age or a post-literate society,' says a sixth. 'Not essential for development,' says a seventh.

There is an element of truth and falsehood in each statement. But are literacy enthusiasts in danger of making exaggerated claims as to its value? Or are the sceptics paying too much attention to facts and figures and missing out on some of the emotional and psychological factors? And who is to challenge the 'received wisdom'?

Arguments Against

First, research has shown, for example, that it is too simplistic to suggest that illiteracy and poverty inevitably go hand in hand, or that the ability to read and write is necessary for development, or that becoming literate will of itself make a person more critical or analytical.

Second, anthropologists and sociologists, after studying literacy practices in a variety of locations over the last ten years, can now demonstrate how the practices vary sufficiently from place to place to challenge the traditional view that literacy is a single, uniform skill, essential to functioning in modern society.

Third, before making too many generalizations it is important to define what is meant by literacy.

Figures from ALBSU (the Adult Literacy and Basic Skills Unit) in 1993 show that 13% of adults in the UK have serious difficulties with reading, writing and basic mathematics, and include those who can barely read at all, those who can read a little (hesitantly), and those who can read fairly well but have great difficulty with writing, particularly spelling. Many find even the simplest calculations difficult and the problems are not confined to any particular age group or geographical area.

ALBSU therefore defines 'basic skills' as the ability to read, write and speak and use mathematics at a level necessary to function and progress at work and in society in general. In some developing countries, however, literacy may mean the ability to write your name, or it may refer to functional literacy, which again may mean the three R's or the three R's plus an ability to extend horizons and improve the quality of life. It is therefore very important to know what we are talking about when we use the term.

Fourth, some women writers, like Barbara Rogers and Jane Bonnick, are critical of the colonial rule which created male hierarchies whilst female hierarchies atrophied or were actively suppressed, 'particularly by missionary organizations' imposing Western concepts which led to the domestication of women. After examining an experimental project to combine functional literacy and non-formal education, for rural women in India, conducted by the Indian Council for Social Development in a drought-prone district of Andra Pradesh, 1972-1975, Bonnick shows how the functional literacy aspect of the project served as a tool to perpetuate the woman's subordinate position in society; moreover, because its central concern was to enable women to improve their ability in bringing up children it made almost no attempt to build on the reading and numerical skills which they already had and thus failed to bring about the changes in health education that the project organizers hoped for.

Fifth, other writers and researchers have been critical of the way literacy campaigns have been used by some, though by no means all, religious organizations as a means of proselytization. Some religious groups concentrate on reading and writing and encourage students to read widely and develop every aspect of their being. Others, however, of a certain theological persuasion, tend to exploit literacy courses, so that what passes for literacy work is little better than using religious literature to proselytise, and there are even those who openly major on the Bible and religious literature from the start and simply hope that by the end their students have picked up the rudiments of reading. Depending on your viewpoint all three approaches can be justified, but it does need to be clear what sort of course is being pursued.

Positive Values

There are two arguments which most literacy teachers would regard as myths and want to kill off immediately.

First, that literacy training is more important in countries with a high degree of illiteracy than in those with a low. The argument is bewitching by its simplicity and the way it is expressed. It is part of the 'go where the need is greatest' argument. But it begs the question as to where the need is greatest. Societies with a high degree of illiteracy operate in other ways and have other (often more traditional) ways of communicating and the illiterate are not necessarily isolated. Societies with a low level of illiteracy, on the other hand, depend on reading as the main form of communication. Anyone who cannot read feels both isolated and diminished as a person. Literacy is not just about reading. It is about self-esteem and one's place in society.

Second, that reading is less important as we move into an electronic society. This 'myth' has been around for forty years since William Gray cited radio broadcasts alongside other aids to learning such as demonstrations, posters and films as being far more effective than the traditional literacy view which believed that the ability to read and write was the first step in helping people to face their problems intelligently, to improve their health and their economic and social status, and to enrich their lives. Gray, however, did go on to point out that it was an extreme view, that the methods were not mutually exclusive and that sooner or later reading was essential to the promotion of human welfare.

Most committed literacy teachers would accept his final comment and suggest to any who doubted that they might pursue their own lines of enquiry.

There is little evidence in the West, for example, that the electronic methods of communication are killing the reading habit. Indeed, the more electronic we become and the more complicated society and communication develop, the more important reading and writing are. Anyone who has recently purchased a new video or PC will wonder how they could possibly handle any modern media without the capacity to read. Even if radio and television are simple, how else do you know what is on, where, and when? And since most Third World television comes in English, doubters might try watching a film in a foreign language without benefit of subtitles.

But more important than any of these is that, in a world society which is literate, to deny literacy to any group is to condemn its people to isolation in the world with all the shame, horrors and dangers that such illiteracy would bring. Illiterate people are at a permanent disadvantage, whether as individuals, groups or nations. And at the same time literacy teachers, teachers of slow-learners in UK schools and the experience of dyslexics all testify to the change that comes about in people once the reading habit has been grasped. [8.1]

LEARNING TO READ
in Zimbabwe

International Literacy Day falls in September. It provides an ideal opportunity to reflect on, and identify with, people round the world for whom literacy is not simply a matter of learning to read and write but a matter of independence, self-esteem and social standing.

Organizations like the Adult Literacy Organization of Zimbabwe use it as an occasion to celebrate, to reward those students who have struggled with their letters, to pay tribute to literacy teachers, to gain some publicity for their work and to encourage those unable to read and write to join classes. For those within striking distance celebration means a visit to the Kambuzama Literacy Centre some twenty miles outside Harare.

On this day, the teacher, a young married woman with a family, is not teaching but demonstrating. Together with her students she is showing a number of distinguished visitors, especially those responsible for funding, what the organization does and how it does it. Through an Exhibition Class potential students are encouraged to sign up for the next course. Older hands are expected to say something about the impact which learning to read had had on their lives.

Mary

Mary is one. She was never allowed to go to school. When she asked her father to send her he just brushed her aside. Education was not for girls. Her father's brother told him, 'Don't let her go to school — if you do she'll end up a prostitute', and if the connection was not immediately obvious to everyone there was no doubt that all the African women present understood only too well.

When Mary grew up she met one of her friends with a book and asked her where she had been. 'To school' came the reply. This opened her eyes. A school for adults! She told her husband, who in her case was sympathetic. Even finding the meeting place without being able to read the sign outside was a problem, but in the end she found the teacher next door and registered. At that point she couldn't even tell an A from a B, though to begin with she felt so ashamed she claimed that she could.

She recalled how she had felt embarrassed at a city bus stop. She had to ask people in the queue where it was going. She could hear them saying, 'Fancy you, a well-dressed woman — where were you when all the others went to school?' 'Now I no longer have the problem,' she said. 'Last year I went to Botswana and signed all my own Travellers' Cheques — and any other documents.'

Esther

Esther was one of the fortunate ones who got to school, but when she left she still couldn't read. She managed to get a job in the city, but her illiteracy meant she could never perform as well as she wanted, and she always suffered the indignity of her pay being given to her husband.

She then learned of classes designed to enable poor, rural women to achieve basic literacy. The time taken was anything up to two years. Stage I was to enable women who had never been to school to learn to read and write Shona, with letter-writing an important component, as she was later to discover at great personal cost. Stages 2 and 3 were for Shona and English. This was the stage Esther had reached.

118

Attending classes had never been easy, due partly to domestic crises and partly to male attitudes, but she stuck at it. At one stage she sold vegetables to keep going, but when she mastered the art she felt she had become a more independent person.

Male attitudes in general in Zimbabwe were not so much indifferent as hostile. One student who attended regularly admitted that her husband had no idea what she was doing and would forcibly prevent her if he ever found out. Most men didn't want their wives learning to read. Politicians, mostly male, were not over enthusiastic about encouraging and financing classes, and after watching the drama it was not difficult to see why.

It was a typical piece of African drama, based on Esther's experience, and the high point of the day. Exuberance was unrestrained and there were frequent eruptions into typically African song, dance or ululation. The message was loud and clear.

The Drama

It began with a postman delivering a letter to an illiterate village woman. Because she could not read it she left it for her husband. When he opened it he told her that it was from the furniture suppliers, who were coming to re-possess everything because they had not paid for it. Next day, distraught, she shared her problem with a friend who had learned to read. She showed her the letter. Her friend immediately sized up the situation and explained. This was no letter from the furniture company. It was in fact from her husband's girl friend. She was pregnant. She needed him to come at once and help with the baby. In her distress the poor offended wife went off to the witch doctor who confirmed the story and told her that before long she would be divorced. And the drama ended with a song which pointed out that the moral of the story was that women who did not learn to read would be divorced by their husbands.

Light-hearted and fun, of course! But deadly serious too!

LISA IN BANGLADESH

LISA is not an individual. LISA stands for Local Initiative Support Action, a self-help literacy programme in Bangladesh. After looking at their work the Overseas Development Administration reported that women's lives in Bangladesh are changing as a result of such activity.

Fewer women use thumbprints. Many more read documents and check the small print before signing, sign their name on voters' lists, take more interest in health and in their children's education, and feel a new sense of pride and self-confidence.

They also demand higher wages, largely because most reading groups run savings committees and women now have money of their own.

Muslim men in Bangladesh, unlike some of their Christian male counterparts in Zimbabwe, also seem to react more positively to their wives' literary aspirations. They insist that they learn too, almost as if they are afraid of being left behind!

If that means classes in the evening, which it does, 'no problem,' say the men. If evenings in Bangladesh are dark, which they are, 'no problem,' say the men. If rural areas have no light and no power, which they haven't, 'no problem,' say the men. 'We bring our kerosene lamps and do the best we can.' And they do.

Besides running reading groups LISA publishes reading primers, beginning with the alphabet, the numbers and key words. At the second stage the breadth of the programme is demonstrated by books on health, environment, development, and matters of interest in everyday life. [8.2]

DON'T PUT YOUR DAUGHTER INTO SCHOOL, MRS WORTHINGTON!

The African saying, 'If your sister goes to school your next meal will be her fountain pen', recounted by the French historian René Dumont, shows how far there is still to go, while stories of women attending literacy classes with a swollen face or a badly damaged nose after being severely beaten up by a husband who found her reading, have only too many echoes from women in countries as far apart as Nigeria and Bangladesh who in turn do not want their maids to go to school, preferring to keep them as virtual slaves.

> 'There are, it is true, considerable numbers of matters where practical action is delayed by the absence of sufficient knowledge. There are more, perhaps, where our knowledge is sufficient to occupy us for the next twenty years, and where the continuance of social evils is not due to the fact that we do not know what is right, but to the fact that we prefer to continue doing what is wrong. Those that have the power to remove them have not the will, and those who have the will have not, as yet, the power.' (R. H. Tawney).

Victoria Brittain says Tawney could have been writing about women, poverty and power.

Girls and women score poorly against males in every indicator of development: literacy, school enrolment, attendance at clinics, earnings per hour, access to land, access to credit, access to political power. Of the 960 million illiterates in the world, two thirds are women; of the 130 million children deprived of primary education, 81 million are girls.

Discrimination begins from before birth, when tests to determine the sex of the child may be used to de-select girls and abort them.

By the time they are a little older the discrimination takes another form, with girls between six and nine in Nepal, for instance, working three hours a day in the house compared to their brothers' two hours and, for the next four years, working twice their brothers' three hours. This is their apprenticeship for life as an adult woman, where work begins before dawn and ends after dark — a 68 hour week for women in Africa, 62 hours in Asia, 49 in Europe — against 43 hours worked by Western men.

In Bangladesh, illiteracy — along with the baby boom — is the biggest hurdle to development and future prosperity.

Only three in ten of the country's ninety million adults can read and write. School enrolment record is one of the worst in the world. Although 70% of six-year-olds sign up for school, less then 15% complete five years of primary education. For girls, the figure drops to a staggering 3%.

The adult literacy rate in Bangladesh is currently little more than one third of the population (in the UK it is 99%), but female illiteracy still lags behind at just 22% — only one in seven girls between the ages of 11 and 16 is enrolled in secondary schools. The Government has a target for the year 2000 of 95% gross enrolment in education for both sexes, with 70% completing their education. A substantial problem remains the provision of teachers — at primary level, there is only one for every 62 children, though the ratio at secondary level is as low as 1:30. [8.3]

120

IRENE IGHODARO

Irene Ighodaro, who died recently at the age of seventy nine, was an exception.

Born in Freetown, Sierra Leone, in a society which had produced its first graduate (her husband) only a few years before, she belonged to an eminent family. Her great uncle had read law at Oxford and qualified as a doctor in Edinburgh. For three decades her father was the only black head of a public service department. She grew up mixing with diplomats, politicians, academics and medical colleagues.

She qualified as a doctor at Durham Medical School in 1945, the first African woman to qualify as a doctor in the UK, becoming Sierra Leone's first woman doctor and Black Africa's second female doctor. But was never allowed to forget the fact that in a patrilineal and hierarchical society she was also female .

Much of her working life was in Nigeria, where the test of a woman's worth was her ability to produce children. Between 1952 and 1958, thanks to her husband's moves, she had to start her practice three times from scratch. On one occasion, when she tried to register to vote, she was refused on the grounds that women did not pay tax. she insisted on paying tax and voting. She set up the University of Benin's teaching hospital and became the first Chairman of the Board — the first time a woman had been appointed to so high a policy-making position in Nigeria.

Throughout she never failed to use an opportunity to mobilize women into new and effective organizations, and over fifty years established an international reputation as a speaker for, and exponent of, the rights and potential of African women.

When she died in 1996 she had an obituary in *The Guardian*. [8.4]

DISADVANTAGES OF ILLITERACY

Unable to turn to books for inspiration and knowledge.

In danger of being duped by rogues.

Cannot apply to authority in writing to redress grievances.

Cannot read regulations, labour contracts, names of roads and stations, safety signs.

Cannot write home when travelling, except through a third party.

Suffer limited economic opportunities because many occupations are closed to them. [8.5]

* * * * * * *

'The real tragedy is that (people unable to read and write) have no voice in public affairs, they never vote, they are never represented in any conference, they are the silent victims, the forgotten men, driven like animals, mutely submitting in every age before and since the pyramids were built.' [8.6]

* * * * * * *

International Literacy Year will not mean very much until politicians put the subject high on the political agenda. One of the problems is that politicians are not very interested in it, and the position will not change until they are competing with one another to see who has the most literate constituency. [8.7]

BIBLES FOR ROMANIA

Whilst some fear the art of reading, others fear the freedom of the press.
Always a live topic in Eastern Europe, and not least under Communism,
the issues are not always what they seem

The dangers for believers who regard themselves as the sole guardians of truth, and then designate all who choose a different path as heretics at worst and sects at best, is illustrated by Romania's problems under Communism with the shortage of Bibles.

The dominant church in Romania at that time was the Orthodox. It was the largest, had the closest contact with the government, was responsible for all Christian publishing, including Bibles, and had its own printing house. The fastest growing, on the other hand, was the Baptist church, many of whose converts were former Orthodox members, if not always Orthodox believers and practitioners.

Naturally the Orthodox resented the Baptists, whom they regarded as a sect, and though the leadership at the top managed to maintain a reasonable relationship, it was a very different story in the villages. Catholics in Northern Ireland, Protestants in France and not a few nonconformists in English villages where the parish priest regards everyone as 'belonging to him' will know the feeling. The Bible was often the battleground, which explains why there were so many stories in the 1980s about Bible smuggling.

What was the problem? Was there really a shortage of Bibles? 'Yes', said the Baptists. 'No', said the Orthodox. 'We print them and publish them. They are openly on sale in our bookshops and customers are never asked questions about their churchmanship.' Both were right and both were wrong. Three factors need to be remembered.

First, the Orthodox Church by its very nature depends less on the Bible in the pew than do the Protestant churches.

Second, the Protestant churches are growing rapidly and the Orthodox Church finds the rapid growth uncomfortable.

Third, none of the Romanian churches is used to the multiplicity of translations that we have had to get used to in the last thirty years.

But the real problem had to do with the Romanian Bible. Romania had two Bibles, the Orthodox Bible and the Protestant Bible, and they quarrelled over them in much the same way as Catholics and Protestants used to fight over who had the true version in this country half a century ago?

The Orthodox Printing House, legally responsible for Bible production, refused to print the Protestant Bible, translated in the 1920s by Dumitri Cornilescu, on the grounds that it was 'too modern' and 'contained inaccuracies'. The Protestants, on the other hand, rejected the Orthodox Bible because it used 'priest' instead of 'elder' or 'presbyter', and so on. What was needed was a new translation by professional scholars, Orthodox and Protestant, using original texts and comparing versions. In fact, a Romanian *Good News Bible,* a *New Revised Standard (or Common)Version.*

Perhaps one day it will happen. Meanwhile, Protestants are well aware of the sales resistance to be overcome to establish such a new version and were not a little daunted at the thought of purchasing 120,000 new Bibles for Baptists alone.

Some Orthodox sources seemed to think that was not a high price to pay for a more satisfactory version of the Bible all round, though recognized it would be a long and laborious task — at least five years, and some would have put it at ten.

SOME POST-PENTECOSTAL QUESTIONS

Pentecost declared God's will to create a unity based on a common purpose. To what extent have we developed that intention and to what extent have we helped ourselves?

Colonialization may have begun as an attempt to create a better world but soon became a massive act of self-indulgence and exploitation to create a better world *for me*.

Much early **missionary activity** likewise. Carey's efforts and breadth of vision may have been unquestionable, Schweitzer's perhaps less so, but much missionary activity very quickly became first an extension of the church, then a means of promoting the missionary society, and finally an expression of Western imperialism.

So too, the **aid agencies**, originally extensions of overseas aid (with the governments wanting the aid agencies to do the work and the agencies wanting the government to provide the funding) but then moving inexorably to the point where the emphasis is on the extension of the agency.

What of **the European Community?** The latest attempt to create a new unity for the benefit of the world? Or a rich man's club?

The hermeneutic of suspicion, a legacy of the liberation theology movement, says that traditionally, biblical story and interpretation have been left to the experts — students of philosophy, theology and biblical languages. But if you ask the poor, and the exploited, who never find a place in theological books and journals, you find you get a different set of questions. They ask . . .

1 Why is this story told in this way?

2 Why are these particular people made the central characters?

3 Why has this story been remembered and handed down?

4 What biases does it have?

They are also good questions to ask when confronted with the latest news story or charitable appeal [8.8]

UNICEF says one third of all the world's children are under-nourished

HOW DO YOU WANT THE FIGURES?

35,000 every day — all under the age of five — and from preventable causes linked to hunger and malnutrition? 1.3 million deaths in one year? One every 2.5 seconds? Or . . .

40,000 children died last night, and most of you don't give a shit!. What's worse is that most of you are more offended because I just said 'shit' than because those 40,000 children died. [8.9]

SOME DO'S AND DON'TS FOR GIVING AID

If the aid agencies are to be criticized for their motivation and the way they make their appeals, we the general public (and no less the Christian public) are vulnerable when it comes to our responses.

One of the problems we all have with charitable giving is guilt. Quite apart from the fear that perhaps we are not giving as much as we ought, we know that directly or indirectly we are all in some way responsible for many of the needs and problems that arise.

We know also that there is no way we can help them all and that even if we were to sell all we have and give to 'the poor', even with lashings of love and everything but the ultimate sacrifice thrown into the bargain (1 Cor 13: 3), it would still not solve most major problem, 'the poor' would scarcely notice and we could even end up just adding one more name to their list. So we have to stop and think, and fortunately what is good for our soul is also good for charities.

Satisfactory charitable giving depends on a number of carefully thought out decisions. There are four steps worth taking:

1 An adequate and realistic assessment of what we have and what we need.

2 An overall decision as to how much we will give away.

3 An assessment of the charities we wish to support.

4 An allocation of the funds.

If we can do it through a covenant account and so increase our gift from taxable income so much the better. If not, we can put something aside in an account (or in a tin under the bed!) each week so that it is there when we need it. And because we have no idea what sudden emergency or strong appeal is likely to cross our path and pull at our heart-strings we may wish to keep some money unallocated for spontaneous response.

Once our heart is right and we are at peace with ourselves, it is then easier to say no to many of the other appeals which come knocking at the door. Whether it does anything to discourage the multitudinous ways in which we are asked to give, or to reduce the waste in purely emotional and thoughtless giving, or to prevent those charities with the highest profile or the best publicity machine walking off with an undue share of the available charitable resources, is doubtful, but at least it will ease our conscience, especially when we go to church or turn on the radio.

But then when it comes to saying no, how do we do it? One way is to ask questions, find out what is happening and possibly regularly revise our giving and distribution. Here are some simple questions to ask.

1 How many other appeals could I receive just like this and what makes this so special?

2 Who is behind this appeal, and why?

Beware the large appeal agencies with high profile and considerable skill in presenting an appeal in such a way that you feel you just have to give.

Beware the small appeal with no backing more than a local action group just trying to help their friends, near or far. What are the chances of your gift ever getting through and what are the means of accountability?

Don't say, 'It doesn't matter — I only gave a pound!' Bad giving is bad stewardship whatever the amount. It encourages shoddy, ill-thought-out charity, adds to the build-up of 'compassion fatigue' and damages the real needs and the honourable charitable work that ought to be supported.

3 Why am I being 'fed' this particular story? Why this and not that? Why are we suddenly focusing on Ethiopia with mass television coverage when there are equally pressing needs in other parts of the world? Why last year Sri Lanka, this year Somalia, and what will it be next year? And why do we hear of victims and atrocities in Bosnia or Rwanda, but rarely in East Timor, Angola or Pakistan, or whatever?

4 Who is deciding what I see, and why do they want me to see this and not that?

Is it the media who happened to have some television cameras in the right place at the right time, with lots of good pictures for news programmes, until something more interesting turned up?

Is it a story with lots of controversy so that the media can easily keep it in the news or is it one that the public would rather not hear about so that the media will want to drop it as soon as they can?

Is it a charity which has suddenly decided to run a campaign on a particular need or region?

And who decides when to stop and move us on to somewhere else, so that in a month's time the thoughtful will be asking 'Whatever happened to . . . ?' and those whose needs were unfulfilled will be left wondering why the flow has suddenly dried up.

5 What vital needs never reach us through television, and why? Is it because they have no pictures to go with them or is it because the pictures are so horrific that they could not be shown?

6 Why do some needs (such as cancer research) gain high profile and consequently high funding whilst others (such as help for the mentally ill)

remain low? And if those are two obvious examples, might it also be the case with less obvious examples. So how do I avoid the pots already being amply filled and find those equally important ones which everyone seems to miss?

Reflecting on these questions will doubtless raise many others. Discussion with friends will produce even more. Workers with charities might be encouraged to join in the discussion because many of them are concerned about the same issues.

MEDIA INFLUENCE

'The world is littered with conflicts which have been forgotten by Western donors. Government aid policies tend to hinge on whether television journalists show interest in a conflict or not.' [8.10]

RELIGIOUS FREEDOM?

So what about church printing presses in the new Russia? Unfortunately these are few and far between. Where they exist they are as busy as the rest and sometimes church relationships can add a heartache to a headache.

One Orthodox bishop, for example (hopefully an exception!) recently acquired a printing press from abroad. He leased it to a state printer in return for 'favoured treatment' for Orthodox productions. He told the printers they could use it for other work when the Orthodox Church didn't want it, 'but not for Baptists and Pentecostals because they are heretics'. [8.11]

BUILDERS TOGETHER

Human Stories combine with Fiction based on Fact to Spell Hope when People Work Together

Whilst scholars, researchers, missionaries and aid agencies debate the value of literacy, those who do the teaching are never short of a tale about what literacy meant to somebody or other. Personal dignity and self-esteem count for more than theories and arguments.

So one teacher will relate how her students found their new knowledge invaluable when travelling and shopping. Another will recall how he encouraged literacy courses in a time of drought because one of the ways of countering the effects of excessive dehydration is constant mental stimulation.

During the Zimbabwe war of independence the Adult Literacy Organization felt compelled to abandon its literacy work. Nobody was interested. Guns, butter and survival were paramount. So they took themselves off to the Red Cross camp outside the city and started a relief job among refugees who had come in from the Bush.

These people had never known a cash economy, but now they had to shop in the supermarket. They had to be able to find what they wanted, read the labels, see the price, check their change and make sense of the cooking instructions when they got it home. Whilst in the camp they found themselves engaging in small businesses and money-making activities, like sewing, making wire netting and selling clothes.

They wanted to continue these occupations once the war ended, so they had to be able to place orders, read letters and contracts, and keep accounts. Learning to read, up to then a luxury, suddenly became the *sine qua non* of survival, and literacy teachers who had gone to the camp for other reasons suddenly found all their skills in great demand.

It was not unlike Father Kovalski in Dominique Lapierre's *The City of Joy*, who wanted to build something together with his fellow men and women in a 'gulag' of Calcutta where 70,000 people were fighting each day for their survival . . . where hundreds died each year of tuberculosis, leprosy, dysentery, and all the diseases caused by malnutrition in this environment so polluted that thousands never reached the age of forty. They needed a dispensary and a leprosy clinic, a home for children with rickets, emergency milk rations for babies and pregnant women, drinking water fountains, more latrines and sewers. The urgent tasks were countless.

So he suggested they should all make an individual survey to discover the most immediate problems the people there wanted to see given priority.

'The results came in three days later. They were all identical. The most pressing desires of the inhabitants of the City of Joy were not the ones that the priest had anticipated. It was not their living conditions that people wanted to change. The sustenance they sought was not directed at their children's frail bodies, but at their minds. The six surveys revealed that the primary demand was for the creation of a night school so that children employed in workshops, stores and tea shops in the alley could learn to read and write.'

Similarly, evidence from the Ghanaian Functional Literacy Programme shows how religious reading material was in high demand by the learners despite the fact that the Ministry of Education were promoting booklets on more secular themes such as immunization, family planning, income generation and so on. [8.12]

THE CUTTING EDGE

The Adult Literacy Organization of Zimbabwe stands firmly on a Christian foundation, with headquarters in Harare. Its roots go back over sixty years.

Its primary commitment is to enable adults to read and write so as to exercise a fully human role in a literary society. Its secondary purpose is to become self-sufficient.

ALOZ lives with three over-riding problems.

1 Persuading people to want to give money for literacy.

2 Convincing people that the stigma of illiteracy is more than an inability to read.

3 Avoiding preoccupation with the middle classes and appreciating the limitations which illiteracy breeds.

Its work and objectives over the years include:

1 Training adult literacy tutors, designing and producing literacy materials, providing literacy programmes.

2 Basic adult education to improve the quality of life in Zimbabwe's citizens.

3 Promoting the social, economic, cultural, political and intellectual development of literacy students through

(a) the teaching of particular skills such as communication, record keeping and leadership, and

(b) the encouragement and practice of self-reliance activities, savings clubs and income-generating projects.

4 Enhancing the professional development of literacy teachers and the quality of literacy instruction through training, refresher courses, supervision of literacy programmes, testing of literacy students and evaluation of such programmes.

The Organization depends on its donors for funding, and on its students, teachers, staff and Board for vision, reliability and co-operation.

THE CHANGING FACE

Hongkong Baptist Theological Seminary was founded by the Hongkong Baptist Convention in 1951 to train ministers and provide theological training for pastors forced out of China after 1949.

Today there are over 100 students and a faculty of 16, half of whom hold doctorates, with only 5 expatriates. Faculty have study leave for 6-8 months every 4 years.

The library has over 30,000 titles, half in Chinese and half in English, and nearly 400 periodicals, a quarter of them Chinese, with a claim of more than 5% of the total seminary budget.

Besides the usual theological training there are full programmes in Christian education and music and occasional courses on specific subjects such as women's ministry and world religion. The normal length of a full course is 3 years and the curriculum is reviewed every 5 years.

Relationships with the local community, secular and ecclesiastical, are good.

The seminary is one of the five founding members of the Hongkong Theological Education Association and all faculty members are assigned to local churches where they act as advisers to ministers.

A NEW WORLD

A serious approach to the questions of aid matters and the developing world, even if it amounts to no more than raising questions, inevitably leaves you with the feeling that nothing is right. First World attitudes are clearly not right. Third World attitudes are intractable. Aid Agency attempts at 'handling and solving' are unsatisfactory and cannot be made satisfactory by tinkering or even by major surgery. What is needed is nothing less than a New World in which we can all share as equals. And that too is unrealistic this side of the grave.

But then so is the gospel! And so is the kingdom! Eden has gone. New heaven and new earth are not yet. Meanwhile we need ways of regularly perceiving that other world and moving into it, even if only temporarily. The horizons need to merge — often — even if they separate again soon afterwards.

One way is to try a literary reading of Isaiah 53 which in this context may help us to come to new insights relating to aid and the developing world but which, once executed, may also provide us with a tool for 'other worlds' we would like to explore.

Isaiah 52: 13 - 53: 12 is a classical poem of the Old Testament. It is read and sung at Easter and Christmas and most believers have put their own Christian interpretation on it.

First, try looking at some of the things you may have missed.

1 Silence is kept, speech is avoided. Nobody says anything. There is a 'report' (53: 1) but we have no idea what it said. Twice we are told of the Servant that 'he did not open his mouth' (53: 7). There is nothing to hear. Only something to see. So what do we see and what does it 'say'?

2 There are no feelings. Hebrew poetry is full of 'feeling' words (cf Isa. 54) but this poem has none. We don't know how Yahweh, the 'we' or the 'they' feel about the Servant, and the Servant seems to have not to have any feelings at all. He scarcely exists (53: 3). Therefore the reader has to imagine the feelings. Role play them.

Second, try to appreciate those interpreters who say that language doesn't have to be talk *about* something. Language can actually *do* something.

So instead of asking what the words 'say' ask what they 'set going'.

Notice, for example, how in this poem, rather like Alice in *Alice in Wonderland*, language actually creates an alternative world which destroys the validity of the conventional world we are familiar with and invites us to enter the new one.

This is a world you cannot view from the outside, as a spectator. You can only appreciate it by being in it. Once there, reader and text are no longer subject and object. Text has power over reader.

Nor can you continue to talk about 'the meaning' as if it only had one. Meaning lies in what it becomes for you, the reader, and with multiple readers we have multiple meanings.

But because we cannot change worlds all at once there has to be this 'merging of horizons', often temporary and always gradual, which means that initially all that the new world may do is enable you better to appreciate the old world.

When Philip expounds this new world for the Ethiopian, for example, he is not laying down some definitive Christian interpretation but expounding one of many meanings and perhaps even encouraging us to find our own (Acts 8: 26ff.). His words are not intended 'to say something' (i.e. convey one message) but 'to do something' (i.e. create another world for us).

Third, with this understanding, explore three further areas in this strange new world.

1 Following a careful reading of this shocking poem make a list of the characteristics of this topsy-turvy world we are invited to enter where everything is called in question:

> where servants and slaves are elevated above kings.
>
> where one achieves what the many cannot.
>
> where the 'intercession' of one avails for the many (v 12).
>
> where God designates his servant and hero as an object of loathing.
>
> where the servant of God practises non-violence and never speaks dishonestly (v 9) but still finishes up in the condemned cell.
>
> where the suffering of the righteous man is the will of God (v 10).

2 'Paint a picture' (in words) of the *dramatis personae*:

(a) 'They'. These are observers, not committed, who find the history of the servant unbelievable and his aspect revolting. They ponder and see his fate. Yet they are fascinated by him and in the end do at least begin to appreciate what he has done for them (vv 11-12).

(b) 'We'. These started like the 'they' but soon saw that the suffering of the innocent was because of, for the sake of, or on behalf of themselves. Their eyes were opened (v 5). They are 'in the poem', have begun to appreciate the new world and see that things are not what they seem.

(c) 'The Servant'. This is the one who grabs the reader, gives him a new understanding of himself and of the direction of his life. He interprets the reader — the reader doesn't interpret him. He destroys an old world and creates a new one.

Fill out the picture of the Servant and especially those characteristics which strike chords for you:

> e.g. he does nothing and says nothing but lets everything happen to him — he is acted upon more than he acts
>
> his actions are negative (he opened not his mouth) or passive (he bore the punishment)
>
> he suffers, but not in any striking way.

Fourth, try to identify the three groups (remember the Servant doesn't have to be an individual) in today's society, and because we are concerned with aid matters think in aid terms. Think of classes, castes, tribes, ethnic groups and whole countries.

Finally, paint a picture of this world you feel you are being drawn into.

Questions

1 Is your picture a picture of the old world or the new world?

2 Where do you see yourself? Where are you? Where would you like to be?

3 Who and where is 'the Servant' for you? For whom and where are you the Servant?

4 What do we do with 'the Servant'? Are we all meant to be like that? Can we live like that all the time?

5 What will 'the Servant' do with us? [8.13]

HOW LISA CHANGED A LIFE

Anwara is a thirty year-old woman who lives in a rural village in Bangladesh.

She is the eldest daughter of a poor farmer. Despite her keen interest in study she had to work in the field along with her father and brothers, and had no access to school.

When she was only thirteen, Anwara got married and lost all opportunity to study because of household work in her husband's family. After she bore two children, she lost her husband. In the absence of an earning member of the family she also had to take responsibility for earning for the family. She says, 'When I saw a literate mother I thought to myself, "I will never be able to read or write".'

One day Umma Kulsum, a teacher at a LISA centre, met Anwara and said, 'Auntie, LISA has started a literacy class for thirty of the illiterate women in the village. Why don't you join in? They will supply all the materials, and if you enrol you will be able to read and write, and you will come to know much more about the world.'

Anwar was interested and enrolled on the LISA course. Since then she has worked hard to improve her literacy skills. Now she can read books, write letters and keep accounts. She can join other women in planning improvement to the village or in developing income-generating schemes.

She is free from the curse of illiteracy and advises other women in her village to go to school. She says, 'It is possible to take away wealth but the education one receives cannot be taken away.' [8.14]

Things to Do

A CELEBRATION

Use International Literacy Day (or some other day if that is more convenient) to focus attention on literacy by creating a celebration event.

Begin with an appreciation of reading and literature. Invite people to read a favourite paragraph or poem and say why it is important to them. If the community is large and the publicity strong why not arrange for certain kinds of literature to be 'read' at certain hours and encourage people to drop in when convenient.

Create a display of the different kinds of reading material with which we are all familiar, but which we are liable to take for granted, with a few 'pointers' to how different life might be if reading were not a possibility.

Encourage a few people to make a presentation to demonstrate what it is like to be living in a community where most people can read but you can't. Help people 'to feel themselves' into the reality of illiteracy.

Try to capture the thrill of an adult who is illiterate in the moments when reading and writing become a normal part of life. One way of doing this might be to invite a local teacher who has specialized in helping pupils with learning difficulties, particularly reading difficulties: they usually know what it means to pupils when they break through.

Provide a few up-to-date statistics on literacy in your community compared to literacy in some of the poorer countries.

Try to work out a few realistic ways in which your community could do something to help an overseas literacy organization like LISA in Bangladesh or ALOZ in Zimbabwe. Further information is available on such organizations from mission and aid agencies.

DISADVANTAGES OF ILLITERACY

Enter into conversation, personally or in a group, with a teacher of children with learning difficulties, a teacher of literacy to adults or someone with experience of teaching victims of dyslexia. After talking about the mechanics of learning to read and write, encourage the teachers to talk about the emotional problems that go with the disability: the shame, the fear, and so on and the thrill once the battle is won.

Invite other people to enter into different experiences imaginatively. Jot down how much more difficult life would be if you could neither read nor write:

> e.g. shopping, getting money, buying a house, getting news or information, planning a holiday, keeping in touch with friends and family, making appointments, visits to doctors, dentists, etc, simple travel. Add to the list as you wish.

Braver people might spend a couple of hours in a city pretending to be illiterate to see how it feels:

> e.g. ask someone the number of the bus as it arrives, a waiter to read a menu, ask which is the ladies and which is the gents, or which floor Fashion is on when you are gazing at the Floor Guide.

Experiment with simple copying of unfamiliar words and letters. Give a passage in a foreign language (Polish or Hungarian if you get it) to half-a-dozen people and ask them to copy it. How many get it all correct first time? Try pronouncing some of the words to sense the problems of correlation between what is seen and what is heard.

Finally, share your feelings. Draw up a check list of the disadvantages of illiteracy and compare it with the one on p. 129. Pray for people who have to live with the problems and emotions you have experienced, and for those who spend so much time trying to help them.

EYES TO SEE

Of all the international news in the press 90% comes from, four or five big Western news agencies. Television draws on the same sources with similar, if not the same, results.

None of the agencies can determine what happens but they can certainly determine the way in which it is presented, and press and television editors can determine whether it is presented at all, how much, how often, and with what depth. In television terms, items which can be presented visually are more likely to receive coverage than those which can't.

Explore these strengths and weaknesses in general with a view to being more alert when there are national or international disasters. Privately, or in a small group, try training your eye on the TV and asking questions, like who decides what we see and why, and how we discover the truth of what we being offered on the box.

Practise evaluating news bulletins. News is never straightforward. It has to be selective. It is influenced by the people who make it, whether they are reporters or interviewers. It is influenced by the editor who determines what we see, what we don't see and in what order we see.

Or learn to look critically at documentaries, particularly those relating to aid and the developing world. A good documentary should tell you something you didn't know before and enable you to enter into the feelings of the people in the story, but never forget that the people who make it also have a point of view and a reason for presenting it in the way they do. Nothing is neutral or 'just facts'. Discerning that is an important part of understanding and appreciation.

Having increased your awareness of these issues, take the next national or international disaster and appeal, look at it more critically and encourage others to do the same.

Food for Thought — Food for Prayer

FOOD PRODUCTION

Give thanks because 1984-94 saw the world's food production increase by 24% — faster than the population growth.

Remember the needs of people in the developing countries, where (even if fertility rates continue to fall) 3.5bn people will still be added to the world's population in the next 30 years and life expectancy, which has risen from 41 to 61 in the past 40 years, is expected to continue to rise.

Remember the needs of people in the industrialized countries whose share of the population will shrink and age — UN forecasts suggest that the proportion of people over 65 will rise from 12.6%-18.4% (1994-2025) — and imagine the strain this will put on natural resources (forests, fish, clean air, etc).

Remember the victims of child deaths and their families.

LITERACY TEACHERS

Literacy teachers are the frontline of the literacy movement, with a burning commmitment to the importance of the word, written and read, and the needs of their pupils. But they are dependent for their bread and butter on other literacy workers raising the funds.

Pray for them and their families as they live with this tension.

Category

Magazines and Newspapers

Remember

Journalists, editors, printers
all-night drivers, distributors, newsagents
delivery boys and girls

Focus On

a situation when you depended on the press
for the truth. Give thanks for its existence,
its freedom, its quality of production
and its faithful arrival

PRINTING PROBLEMS

Spare a thought for Christian writers, publishers and editors who have to negotiate in poor countries with state or privately owned commercial printing presses and who find that their Christian work is often pushed to the back of the queue because commercial interests, and sex and pornography in particular, pay better.

Try to appreciate the problems this causes for a weekly or monthly publication: broken deadlines, unreliable disribution and delivery times, bad reputation, loss of sales, declining advertising income, uncertain cash flow, threat of closure.

Now pray for the staff and their families.

Pray for Librarians and their Libraries

at home as well as overseas.

Imagine their problems

SOURCES AND RESOURCES

Advent

1.1 For further discussion of these issues see P. T. Bauer, *Equality, the Third World and Economic Delusion,* Weidenfeld and Nicolson 1981 (especially chapter 5), Gerald M. Meier, *Leading Issues in Economic Development,* Fourth Edition, Oxford University Press 1984, pp. 293-4, and John Toye, *Dilemmas of Development,* Blackwell 1987, pp. 5ff.

1.2 Susan George, *How the Other Half Dies. The Real Reasons for World Hunger,* Penguin Books 1976, p. 17.

1.3 From 'Giving a Voice to the Silent Majority' by John Pilger, in *The Guardian,* 25 February 1997.

1.4 Michael Bourdeaux, *Gorbachev, Glasnost and the Gospel,* Hodder & Stoughton 1990, and Jim Forest, *Free At Last? The Impact of Perestroika on Religious Life in the Soviet Union,* Darton, Longman and Todd 1990.

1.5 Rudy Boschwitz, who helped to draft the US Farm Act (*The Guardian,* 2 April 1996). The Green Revolution is engineered, funded and promoted largely by the USA, which just happens to be the world's most aggressive food exporter.

1.6 *The Guardian,* 2 April 1996 (including the Monbiot quotation below).

1.7 BBC Report, 5 May 1997.

1.8 *The Guardian,* 31 October 1995.

1.9 Reported in *The Observer,* 6 April 1997.

1.10 George Monbiot, quoted from *The Guardian* (date unknown).

1.11 Michael Taylor, writing in *Missionary Herald,* October 1996.

Christmas

2.1 For further discussion of these issues see Robert Chambers, *Rural Development. Putting the Last First,* Longman, 1983 and Ron O'Grady, *Third World Stopover. The Tourism Debate,* Risk Book Series, WCC Publications 1981.

2.2 Robert Chambers, *Rural Development. Putting the Last First,* Longman 1983, pp. 11-12.

2.3 From *Joyce Grenfell Requests the Pleasure,* Futura Publications 1976, p 264-7, by permission of Feed the Minds.

2.4 Cecil Rajendra, *Songs for the Unsung,* Risk Book Series, WCC Publications 1983, pp. 8-9, quoted in Ron O'Grady, *Third World Stopover. The Tourism Debate,* Risk Book Series, WCC Publications 1981, pp. 8-9. Rajendra is a protest poet who lives in Penang Island, Malaysia's most popular tourist destination.

2.5 Based on 'A Code of Ethics for Travellers' drawn up in 1975 by the Christian Conference of Asia, reported in *Tourism: the Asian Dilemma,* p. 47, and quoted in Ron O'Grady, *Third World Stopover. The Tourism Debate,* Risk Book Series, WCC Publications 1981, pp. 64-5, in the light of discussions between representatives of the Australian Council of Churches and the Indonesian airline, Garuda, who published a modified version and placed it in the seat pocket of its flights to Indonesia.

2.6 Ron O'Grady, *Third World Stopover. The Tourism Debate,* Risk Book Series, WCC Publications 1981, p. 52.

2.7 Ron O'Grady, *Third World Stopover. The Tourism Debate,* Risk Book Series, WCC Publications 1981, p. 25.

2.8 Emmanuel de Kadt, *Tourism — Passport to Development,* UNESCO-World Bank, Oxford and New York 1979, p. 420, quoted in Ron O'Grady, *Third World Stopover. The Tourism Debate,* Risk Book Series, WCC Publications 1981, p. 10.

2.9 Tom Hodkinson, *The Guardian,* 26 August 1997.

2.10 'International Workshop on Tourism' quoted in Ron O'Grady, *Third World Stopover. The Tourism Debate,* Risk Book Series, WCC Publications 1981, p. 34.

2.11 Based on Jean Keefe, 'Holiday Dream Profits', in *Spur* (World Development Movement), March/April 1992.

2.12 H. B. Dehqani-Tafti, *Design of My World,* SPCK 1959.

Lent

3.1 For further discussion of these issues see Robert Chambers, *Rural Development. Putting the Last First,* Longman 1983 and Robert Chambers (ed), *Challenging the Professions,* Intermediate Technology Publications 1993, pp. 1-14.

3.2 John Pilger, *A Secret Country*, Jonathan Cape 1990, pp. 346-7.

3.3 Lynda Chalker, 'Liberty, Equality and Maternity', in *The Observer*, 16 October 1994 (Concern Worldwide Inset, p. 8).

3.4 Robert Archer, 'South Sudan: Making Liberty', in *Viewpoint*, No. 9 (August 1995), Christian Aid.

3.5 Robert Chambers, *Rural Development. Putting the Last First*, Longman 1983, p. 75.

3.6 Vera Brittain, *Testament of Youth*, Virago Press 1978.

3.7 Kahlil Gibran.

3.8 Source unknown.

3.9 Based on figures in *The Guardian*, 5 May 1992.

3.10 Susan George, *How the Other Half Dies. The Real Reasons for World Hunger*, Penguin Books 1976, pp. 289, 296.

Holy Week

4.1 For further discussion of these issues see Susan George, *How the Other Half Dies. The Real Reasons for World Hunger*, Penguin Books 1976, and Frances Moore Lapp and Joseph Collins, *World Hunger — Twelve Myths*, Earthscan 1992.

4.2 Victoria Brittain, 'When Giving is Guilt-Edged', in *The Guardian*, 14 September 1988.

4.3 John Pilger, 'Giving a Voice to the Silent Majority', in *The Guardian*, 25 February 1997.

4.4 Theatre Royal, Brighton, Programme for *Death and the Maiden*, August 1992.

4.5 *The Observer*, 15 August 1993.

4.6 Ariel Dorfman, writing in *The Guardian*, 22 February 1997.

4.7 Ariel Dorfman, author of *Death and the Maiden*, and Caroline Gorst-Unsworth, a psychiatrist with the Medical Foundation for the Care of Victims of Torture, quoted in Theatre Royal, Brighton Programme for *Death and the Maiden*, August 1992.

4.8 Based on *The 10/40 Window*, produced by The AD2000 and Beyond Movement, Colorado Springs.

Easter

5.1 For further discussion of these issues see Walter Brueggemann, *The Land*, Fortress Press 1977, Norman C. Habel, *The Land is Mine*, Fortress Press 1995, Anthony R. Ceresko, *Introduction to the Old Testament. A Liberation Perspective*, Geoffrey Chapman 1992, J.-J. von Allmen, *Vocabulary of the Bible*, Lutterworth Press 1958, and Harper's *Dictionary of the Bible*, Harper & Row 1988.

5.2 Susan George, *How the Other Half Dies. The Real Reasons for World Hunger*, Penguin Books 1976, pp. 30, 43, 46.

5.3 Jean Varnier (Source unknown).

5.4 Jules Feiffer, quoted in John Pilger, *A Secret Country*, Jonathan Cape 1990, p. 313

5.5 Susan George, *How the Other Half Dies. The Real Reasons for World Hunger*, Penguin Books 1976, pp. 34-6.

Post-Easter

6.1 For further discussion of these issues see Anthony R. Ceresko, *Introduction to the Old Testament. A Liberation Perspective*, Geoffrey Chapman 1992, Dominique Lapierre, *The City of Joy*, Arrow Books 1985, and John Pilger, *A Secret Country*, Jonathan Cape 1990.

6.2 Words attributed to a Brazilian archbishop, struggling shoulder to shoulder with the poor, in Dominique Lapierre, *The City of Joy*, Arrow Books 1985, pp. 419-20.

6.3 Words attributed to Kovalski, the Roman priest anxious 'to build something together' among the poor of Calcutta, in Dominique Lapierre, *The City of Joy*, Arrow Books 1985, pp. 44-5, 49, 372-3.

6.4 John Pilger, *A Secret Country*, Jonathan Cape 1990, p. 35.

6.5 Zimbabwe Christian Leader.

6.6 John Carrington, *The Talking Drums of Africa*, Carey Kingsgate Press 1949.

Pentecost

7.1 For further discussion of these issues see Geoffrey Curtis CR, *Paul Couturier and Unity in Christ*, SCM Press 1964, A. M. Allchin, *The Abbé Paul Couturier*, Faith Press 1960 and Maurice Villain SM, *Abbé Paul Couturier*. Translated by the Sisters of the Holy Cross Convent, from the French *Témoignages*, Haywards Heath 1959.

7.2   The *Observer*, 6 April 1997.

7.3   David Hearst, 'How the East was won — and lost', in *The Guardian*, 19 October, 1996.

7.4   Bob Holman, 'Children in Need of Respect', in *The Guardian*, 19 (or 20) November 1992.

7.5   Susan George, *How the Other Half Dies. The Real Reasons for World Hunger*, Penguin Books 1976, pp. 265-66.

Post-Pentecost

8.1   For further discussion of these issues see Jane Bonnick, 'Women, Illiteracy and Under-development in Rural India: the Limitations of the Autonomous Model', an unpublished paper at the University of Sussex, Alec Gilmore, *Agenda for Development*, SPCK 1996, William S. Gray, *The Teaching of Reading and Writing: an International Survey*, Monographs on Fundamental Education 10, UNESCO 1956, Barbara Rogers, *The Domestication of Women*, Kogan Page 1980, Brian V. Street (ed), *Cross-cultural Approaches to Literacy*, Cambridge University Press 1993 and 'Putting Literacy on the Political Agenda', in *Open Letter*, vol. 1 no. 1, 1990.

8.2   Feed The Minds *News*, August 1996.

8.3   Victoria Brittain, 'Victims from Birth', in *The Observer*, 16 October 1994 (Concern Worldwide Inset, p. 12) and Polly Ghazi, 'Have Schooling, Will Prosper', in *The Observer*, 16 October 1994 (Concern Worldwide Inset, p. 14).

8.4   *The Guardian*, 3 January 1996.

8.5   Margaret Wrong, *West African Journey*, London 1946.

8.6   Frank C. Laubach, *Thirty Years with the Silent Billion*, Lutterworth Press 1961.

8.7   Thérèse Rickman Bull, wife of the Canadian High Commissioner and Acting Director of ALOZ in 1989.

8.8   Anthony R. Ceresko, *Introduction to the Old Testament. A Liberation Perspective*, Geoffrey Chapman 1992, pp. 10ff.

8.9   Dr Tony Campolo, a Baptist minister addressing an audience of British Christians, and quoted by Steve Chalke in *Missionary Herald*, October 1996.

4.10 Cornelio Sammarunga, Head of the International Committee of the Red Cross, reported in *The Guardian*, 14 October 1994.

8.11 A Russian Baptist with a heavy heart but no ill-will.

8.12 Dominique Lapierre, *The City of Joy*, Arrow Books 1985, p. 164.

8.13 I am indebted to David J. A. Clines for the academic background and underlying ideas for this meditation. (See David J. A. Clines, *I, He, We and They. A Literary Approach to Isaiah 53*, Journal for the Study of the Old Testament, Supplement Series 1, Sheffield Academic Press 1976.) Lucky, in Samuel Beckett, *Waiting for Godot*, is so close to the Servant of Isaiah 53 that the play is worth seeing or reading for this alone (see Alec Gilmore, *Preaching as Theatre*, SCM Press, pp. 75-80.)

8.14 Feed The Minds *News*, August 1996.

INDEX

Writers

People, Places and Subjects

Biblical References

Old Testament

Genesis

11. 1-9	97
12-50	67

Exodus

16	13
23. 11	67

Leviticus

23. 36	67
25. 35	67

Deuteronomy

23. 24-25	67

I Kings

21	93

II Kings

5	79

Psalms

8	24
12. 5	67
22. 1	49

Proverbs

13. 23	66

Isaiah

6. 9-10	115
42. 1-6	13
49. 1-6	13
50. 4-9	13
52. 13-53. 12	13, 33, 63, 128f.
54	128

Jeremiah

31. 31-34	14
32. 1-15	14

Daniel

3	60
6	60

Joel

3. 28	111

Micah

3. 1	7

Apocrypha

I Maccabees

2. 29-48	60

New Testament

Matthew

2. 1-11	29
12. 46-50	17
13. 54-58	93
20. 16	33
25. 14-30	61

Mark

1. 2-3	1
2. 1-12	44f.
4. 12	115
6. 1-6	93
6. 3	93
15. 34	49
15. 40-47	78
16. 1-8	78

Luke

2. 1	17, 115
2. 3	17
2. 32	13
2. 35	17
4. 16-29	93
4.18	9, 67
7. 22	67
13. 10-17	45
19. 11-27	61
24. 51	83

John

1. 14	30
3. 16	13
17	110

Acts

1. 9	83
1. 11	83
2. 1-11	111
2. 12	97
2. 13	111
2. 16-36	111
3. 1-10	13
8 . 26-40	92, 129
24. 5	115
26. 7	115
28. 28	115

Romans

13. 1-7	60

I Corinthians

1. 18-31	65, 79
13. 3	124

II Corinthians

12. 10	65, 79

Galatians

3. 28	94

Classification of Topics

The use to which material is put will depend on setting and circumstance
This summary is purely for location purposes

For Reflection and Discussion

Is the Third World the creation of the West and do we need them more than they need us? 2f.

Does foreign travel have any value for understanding and appreciating the lives of other people and their culture? And does it make any difference whether we go as aid agency representatives or simply as tourists? 18f.

A professionalism which is more aware of its own interests and expertise than the needs and abilities of its clients, and what we might do about it 34f.

Does the experience of people who depend on aid at home help us to enter into the feelings of those who depend on aid overseas? And vice versa? 50f.

When did we last stop to think what we meant when we talked about 'the poor'? How does the Bible sharpen our understanding? Who are they and what do they want? 66f., 84f.

What does it mean to share our resources — people with people, churches with churches, agencies with partners? And what are the chances we will ever achieve it? 98f.

How to decide which charities to help 107f.

How important really is literacy? 116f., 120f.

How to evaluate charitable giving and to give without guilt 124f.

Common Mistakes

Free Bibles and old hymnbooks 26

Action without thought, and decisions based more on emotion than reason 27, 30f.

Failing to listen to the local people 36, 58

Some things we never see or hear 87

Throwaway charity 103f.

People on the Move

An Indian doctor who puts the provision of water before hi-tech medicine 8

An Indian civil servant who concentrates on basic sanitation 9

What are the connections between the Wise Men following a star and a twentieth-century child in Persia making a similar journey on the way from Islam to Christianity? 24

The effect of closing the border between China and Hong Kong in 1948 on one young fellow, training for the ministry, and his family 56

A black Zambian, a white Zimbabwean and an educated Filipino: how they were trapped in 'the system' and responded to it 57

The price of illiteracy, the way people take advantage of people who can neither read nor write, and how others respond 69

The value of offering praise and worship to God in your own way, with your own music and your traditional musical instruments, and the commitment of one group of people in Asia to achieve it 70

Thabo Mbeki and the new South Africa 72f.

A Christian Filipino organization committed to basic education for children on the streets whose main obstacle is that they have to work to support their family 100

A Christian Social Laboratory in rural Indonesia evaluates the effect of change on the local community and provides theological education for rural pastors 102

Testimonies to what reading meant to a group of women in Zimbabwe and some Muslim men in Bangladesh 118f.

People under Pressure

Women coping with dependency, violation and the demands of foreign culture 40ff.

Life under a military dictatorship and what it means for theological education and human understanding 52ff.

A Filipino Methodist Superintendent, his commitment to the poor and the price he paid and continues to pay 75

Eastern Europeans in the early 1990s coping with Western-type colonialism 34f.,105

People of Hope

The thirst for literacy and the price some people will pay for it 68

Human beings on the streets of Calcutta and their battle to help themselves by helping others 86

Stories

Third World initiatives in coping with catastrophe 37ff.

One man's vision for a Christian magazine for young people all over Africa, and what he did to achieve it 74

Initiatives that have brought the joy of reading in a variety of ways 88

Religious education when you have no books 89

Listening — and hearing a different language 90

Paul Couturier, the man whose inspiration gave us the Week of Prayer for Christian Unity 101

The deep feelings of the poor 106

What was all that 'fuss' about Bibles for Romania? 122

Literacy as the drive to a fuller life 126